Cambridge Elements

Elements in Applied Evolutionary Science
edited by
David F. Bjorklund
Florida Atlantic University

THE EVOLUTION OF REPUTATION-BASED COOPERATION

A Goal Framing Theory of Gossip

Rafael Wittek
University of Groningen
Francesca Giardini
University of Groningen

Shaftesbury Road, Cambridge CB2 8EA, United Kingdom

One Liberty Plaza, 20th Floor, New York, NY 10006, USA

477 Williamstown Road, Port Melbourne, VIC 3207, Australia

314–321, 3rd Floor, Plot 3, Splendor Forum, Jasola District Centre,
New Delhi – 110025, India

103 Penang Road, #05–06/07, Visioncrest Commercial, Singapore 238467

Cambridge University Press is part of Cambridge University Press & Assessment,
a department of the University of Cambridge.

We share the University's mission to contribute to society through the pursuit of
education, learning and research at the highest international levels of excellence.

www.cambridge.org
Information on this title: www.cambridge.org/9781009462280

DOI: 10.1017/9781009217521

First published 2023

A catalogue record for this publication is available from the British Library

ISBN 978-1-009-46228-0 Hardback
ISBN 978-1-009-21750-7 Paperback
ISSN 2752-9428 (online)
ISSN 2752-941X (print)

The Evolution of Reputation-Based Cooperation

A Goal Framing Theory of Gossip

Elements in Applied Evolutionary Science

DOI: 10.1017/9781009217521
First published online: November 2023

Rafael Wittek
University of Groningen

Francesca Giardini
University of Groningen

Author for correspondence: Rafael Wittek, r.p.m.wittek@rug.nl

Abstract: Gossiping and its reputation effects are viewed as the most powerful mechanism to sustain cooperation without the intervention of formal authorities. Being virtually costless, gossiping is highly effective in monitoring and sanctioning norm violators. Rational individuals cooperate in order to avoid negative reputations. But this narrative is incomplete and often leads to wrong predictions. *Goal Framing Theory*, a cognitive-behavioral approach anchored in evolutionary research, provides a better explanatory framework. Three overarching goal frames (hedonic, gain, and normative) constantly compete for being in our cognitive foreground. This Element argues that for gossip to have reputation effects, a salient normative goal frame is required. But since the hedonic mindset usually trumps gain and normative concerns, most gossip will be driven by hedonic motives and therefore not have strong reputation effects. Propositions on cultural, structural, dispositional, situational, and technological gossip antecedents and consequences are developed and illustrated with evidence from the empirical record.

Keywords: gossip, reputation, cooperation, goal framing, evolution

ISBNs: 9781009462280 (HB), 9781009217507 (PB), 9781009217521 (OC)
ISSNs: 2752-9428 (online), 2752-941X (print)

Contents

1 The Puzzle of Sustainable Cooperation 1

2 The Evolutionary Origins of Gossip, Reputation, and Cooperation 12

3 A Goal Framing Perspective on Gossip, Reputation, and Cooperation 19

4 Gossip: Antecedents and Consequences for Reputation and Cooperation 31

5 Gossip and Reputation in Contemporary Societies 53

6 A Research Agenda for Goal Framing Theory, Gossip, and Reputation Effects 63

References 68

> Gossip is a strange kind of indulgence, the satisfying effect of which consists in the realization that other people do wrong. It gives us pleasure to point out the existence of evil in others. To give vent to that pleasure is gossip. In gossip we are pleased to discuss other people's faults, seldom their merits. We thus seem to enjoy evil for evil's sake. For we are pleased by faults and errors. We are content to see them endure and grow. We are eager to augment their number and to exaggerate their importance. And, mark you, we derive no profit or personal advantage from doing so. If we do, we no longer call it gossip but either libel or slander; gossip is idle and aimless [. . .] gossip is not merely a ludicrous weakness . . . but a social force, an intricate mechanism through which the organized forces of evil gain access to various departments of human life. In the language of theology, . . . gossip may properly be called one of Satan's chief weapons in his design to rule over the world. The Devil has been repeatedly conceived as archgossiper. "How did the Devil fall?" asks Jerome. "Was it after a theft, a murder, an adultery? In truth, these things are sins, but it was not through any of them that the Devil fell. He fell because of his tongue.
>
> Henry Lanz (1936).

1 The Puzzle of Sustainable Cooperation

Gossiping and the reputation effects it produces are widely viewed as the most powerful mechanism to sustain cooperation without the intervention of formal authorities. According to the underlying standard rational choice account, gossiping is an almost costless activity and therefore the ideal instrument to facilitate monitoring and sanctioning of those violating norms (Coleman, 1990). This sanction threat, in turn, increases the likelihood that rational, forward-looking individuals stick to the rules in order to avoid the negative consequences that a bad reputation will bring. The result is a self-reinforcing gossip-reputation-cooperation triangle.

The present Element examines this influential claim in more detail. We argue that this seemingly straightforward narrative and its underlying reasoning is incomplete at best, and in some cases actually leads to wrong predictions. Building on evolutionary research's recent insights into *social* rationality and the importance of so-called *goal frames* (Lindenberg & Steg, 2007), we develop an alternative explanatory framework. This framework acknowledges that evolution equipped humans with a highly flexible and strongly situation-dependent set of three overarching mindsets (or overarching goal frames) that compete for being in our cognitive foreground. These mindsets structure our thinking and strongly influence our motives. The *gain goal frame* – the core assumption of standard rational choice models in economics – is but one of these mindsets. It makes us sensitive to opportunities for improving our resources. The *normative goal frame* – which informs the *Homo socialis* model of most other social science approaches – is another one. It instigates us "do the right thing." Finally, the so-called *hedonic goal frame* triggers us to do what feels good right now. The hedonic goal frame to this point has largely remained under the radar of the science of cooperation in general, and of gossip and reputation scholars in particular. As we will show, this is a major oversight. It is the hedonic mindset that tends to trump gain and normative concerns, unless these receive extra backing from our social environment. This means that most gossip will be driven by hedonic motives, and therefore, we argue, be unlikely to have strong reputation effects. In sum, our goal framing approach yields a variety of new predictions, some of which are at odds with the standard account, but better aligned with the available empirical evidence. It bridges many of the current knowledge gaps and resolves contradictions in the field because it is one of the very few theories of action that is able to reconcile the competing claims about human nature. As a cognitive-behavioral approach anchored in evolutionary research, *goal framing theory* provides a more refined and more accurate psychological microfoundation for the gossip-reputation-cooperation triangle.

Section 1 first outlines the assumptions and propositions behind the "standard" model. This is followed by a description of the fragmented, incomplete, and inconsistent state of the art in the research field. Section 2 gives a summary of current evolutionary approaches to gossip, reputation, and cooperation. It uses Tinbergen's "four questions" to structure the summary. Section 3 introduces the goal framing approach and its core assumptions. Section 4, on gossip and reputation in contemporary society, applies goal framing theory to review current explanations and evidence linking culture, structure, situations, dispositions, and technology to how gossip and reputation may influence cooperation. Section 5 concludes with an exploration of open questions and the contours of a research agenda.

1.1 Gossip and Reputation: Golden Key to Cooperation?

Controversy about gossip, its alleged motives and consequences, and how to deal with them, seem to be a feature of many societies. For some scholars, such as Henry Lanz, the author of the opening quote writing about religion in Western societies, gossip is "Satan's chief weapon," an indulgence that satisfies our lowest desires – such that we derive our satisfaction not from some personal benefit that may come with gossiping, but from the mere pleasure we experience from harming others (Lanz, 1936). Indeed, most cultures have very strong norms against gossiping, especially against women gossiping (Emler, 1994). Islam considers backbiting as the 41st Greater Sin, and also the Bible explicitly condemns gossipers. For example, Psalm 101:5 reads: "Whoever slanders his neighbor secretly I will destroy."

In contrast, there are societies that engage in a far more pragmatic approach when it comes to gossip. In Rome in the first century AD there were enslaved men, such as Aristarchus, who served as *nomenclator* – a "caller of names," or better, a "social secretary." We know about Aristarchus because his patron took the effort to dedicate an epigraph to his nomenclator as an indication of how important Aristarchus' services must have been for him (Wilson, 1910). Nomenclatores played an important role for members of the Roman elite, who often also aspired to make it into powerful political positions. In order to succeed, they needed to solicit support and potential votes from their clients and other influential members. Whenever patrons participated in public gatherings or strolled in public places, their nomenclatores would walk closely behind them. Every time their patron approached someone of importance, the nomenclator would not only remind his patron about the person's name, but also provide relevant evaluative information about their business and current situation, their kinship and social relations, what the patron had done for the client in the past and vice versa. With patrons' networks of clients and supporters going into the hundreds, avoiding the embarrassment of not recalling a client's name was an essential part of keeping one's support relationships going. The role of a nomenclator reflects one of the most institutionalized forms of how a society may regulate and normalize some of the reputation management that is achieved through gossiping.

Gossip as evil, as a sin, or as a powerful political tool nicely capture the multifaceted phenomenon that gossip is, and these quite diverse descriptions also to some degree symbolize the wide gaps that characterize current scholarly endeavors to come to grips with it. These gaps range from assumptions about the motives behind engaging in gossip to its alleged benefits for the individual or the group. But both gossip as sin and gossip as a political tool also share a common message, and this is that we should be aware of the tremendous societal impact that gossip may have. While this insight may be an open door for many, social scientists' awareness of gossip's potentially crucial role is of relatively recent date. For a long time, gossip had not been considered as a topic for serious scientific study, remaining confined to the realm of specialized anthropological case studies (Emler, 1994; Gluckman, 1968). This changed with the 1996 publication of Robin Dunbar's influential book *Grooming, Gossip and the Evolution of Language*. Dunbar's thesis was that gossip evolved as a means that helped human groups to build and cement social bonds without having to directly interact with every other member of their group. This "social grooming" not only played an essential role in the evolution of language – which allows us to share information about third parties – but also to create social order and to sustain cooperation in groups. Dunbar's account provided innovative answers to important questions related to the evolution of gossip (see Section 2 for a detailed discussion). What is gossip's function or adaptive value for humans? How did it evolve in the human species? What are the neurocognitive processes and mechanisms behind it? With Dunbar's contribution, a practice that up until then many had considered as being merely a trivial epiphenomenon of social group processes suddenly had become one of the key levers enabling the evolution of cooperation in human societies.

1.1.1 Cooperation Sustainability Is Key for Society

Cooperation, or the joint realization of mutual benefits, is fundamental for all social species to thrive, and human societies are no exception. It can take many forms. Whether it is about contributing one's fair share to a team effort, about helping your neighbors renovate their kitchen, about paying your taxes, or about volunteering for a nongovernmental organization: it is through cooperation that we can realize outcomes that individual effort alone would never be able to achieve.

Cooperation's importance for society has long been acknowledged, and much scholarship has been devoted to study how to get cooperation going. More recently, the question how to *sustain* cooperation in the longer run has entered center stage.

1.1.2 Current Research Suggests That Gossip and Reputation Solve the Problem of Cooperation Sustainability

Current scholarship considers the opportunity to develop and act upon reputations as the single most important mechanism enabling and sustaining cooperation, including among selfish individuals. The focus on reputation as a major mechanism to enhance cooperation has both theoretical and empirical reasons.

For one, the disciplining effects of reputation can emerge endogenously as the result of the interactions among autonomous individuals. The related processes are self-reinforcing; individuals can freely contribute information to build or break reputations, and no formal centralized sanctioning institutions are required for it to work.

Another reason for the success of reputation is the extensive adoption of online rankings and reputation systems (see Section 5 for a discussion of their relationship with gossip). However, in the offline world, gossip is the way in which reputations are built and destroyed because of its alleged efficiency and effectiveness: gossiping may be almost costless for the gossiper, but it can have a strong impact in reinforcing social norms (Coleman, 1990, pp. 284–285). Without going into definitional issues, it is worth mentioning that there is a remarkable number of different definitions of gossip, as highlighted by a recent systematic meta-review reporting 324 articles from which it is possible to extract a definition of gossip

(Dores Cruz et al., 2021). From this plethora, we select two that are especially relevant for our argument. Gossip is "gossip is the exchange of personal information (positive or negative) in an evaluative way (positive or negative) about absent third parties" -and put "evaluative way" (Foster, 2004, emphasis ours), and a more elaborate account would define gossip as: "sharing evaluative information about an absent third-party that the sender would not have shared if the third-party were present, and which, according to the sender, is valuable because it adds to the current knowledge of the receiver" (Giardini & Wittek, 2019a, p. 2). Both definitions show that gossip is more than knowledge sharing, because what is reported is valuable and it could have been difficult to find out, were the gossip not shared.

However, research on gossip and reputation has mostly focused on gossip as information transmission, developing what we define as "the standard model of reputation-based cooperation." Although very useful in some settings, the standard model does not explain under which conditions gossip does or does not happen, and why it does not work in sustaining value creation. The standard model and its argumentation are simple. In social settings where the transmission or exchange of information about third parties is possible, sharing information about the characteristics of one's interaction partners – such as their reliability or trustworthiness – results in the formation of individual reputations, or shared beliefs about an individual's characteristics (Nowak & Sigmund, 1998, 2005). Such beliefs contribute to a self-reinforcing system of sustained cooperation. The opportunity to select cooperative partners in a "market for cooperators" (Noë & Hammerstein, 1995) and avoid defectors deters potential norm violators because their noncompliance may ruin their reputation, which in turn may deprive them of beneficial exchanges in the future. Reputations therefore work both as an ex ante and an ex post device. The simple possibility or threat that someone might spread negative gossip about our misdeeds would keep us from engaging in them (Piazza & Bering, 2008), and if we do, we will be disciplined by others turning their back on us. The resulting triangle linking reputation and gossip to cooperation sustainability currently constitutes one of the most fruitful theoretical developments in the field of cooperation science (Giardini & Wittek, 2019a; Giardini et al., 2022).

It is important to also highlight four additional assumptions behind this standard model that often remain implicit. First, gossip affects reputations because it transmits accurate (i.e., honest and reliable) information. Gossip veracity is essential for the gossip-reputation-cooperation mechanism to function (Fonseca & Peters, 2018; Nieper et al., 2022; but see Laidre et al., 2013, who argue based on findings from an agent-based model that verifying information with multiple sources can alleviate problems of "noise" in gossip networks). Second, there is a common evaluative reference point that makes it easy to judge when behavior is noncooperative or cooperative. That is, there is a social norm that prescribes or proscribes which behaviors are appropriate or not (Lindenberg et al., 2020). Third, the available evaluations of third parties enforce cooperation because people act upon these reputations, for example by further spreading the information, but most importantly by sanctioning the norm violator (Coleman, 1990). Gossip thereby has the potential to resolve what is known as the second-order free-rider dilemma, according to which sanctioning is costly, and individuals therefore prefer others to do the sanctioning if they benefit from it, as is the case in collective-good situations. Fourth, sharing evaluative information does not have negative consequences for the gossiper (Giardini, 2012; Hauser et al., 2014). Where such antisocial punishment is possible and frequent, for example because the norm violator takes revenge, cooperation declines.

Researchers have accumulated considerable evidence, most of it based on controlled lab experiments, demonstrating that social settings that allow for gathering and sharing information about individual reputations fare much better in sustaining high levels of contributions to collective goods compared to settings in which this information cannot be shared (Milinski, 2019). This standard model of reputation-based cooperation, though, fails in answering two key questions. First, why do people gossip? Even if spreading information about an absent third party can have no immediate costs, still the gossiper can be punished by the target or by the whole group if the intention behind gossip is perceived to be malevolent. Second, the standard model assumes that people have either a selfish motive to spread gossip (to punish the target, to ruin their reputation or their social standing), or an altruistic one, that is, providing norm-abiding behavior and punishing defectors. We will argue in this Element that the whole picture is more complex than this, and that understanding gossip as a goal-driven behavior can shed light on the conditions under which gossip and reputation can sustain cooperation. Figure 1 summarizes the conceptual model behind our argument.

1.2 The Gossip Landscape: Fragmented, Incomplete, and Inconsistent

The gossip-reputation-cooperation triangle underlying the current "standard model" of cooperation assumes a three-step sequence, with each step representing a causal mechanism (see Figure 1):

(1) Cooperative or noncooperative behavior by one party (A) toward another (B) triggers the latter to share positive or negative gossip about A's behavior with third parties (C).

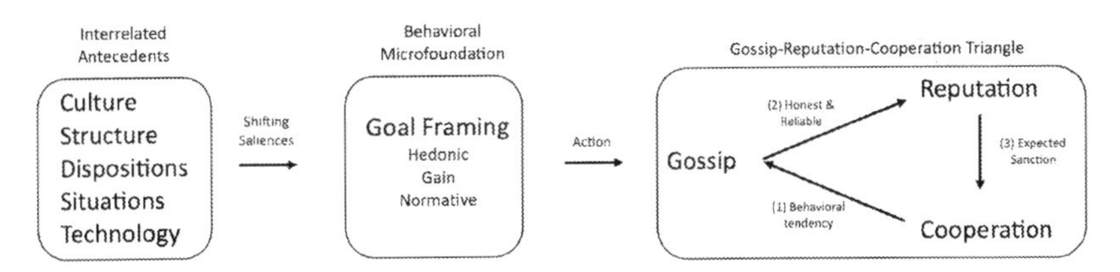

Figure 1 Conceptual model

(2) Gossip, in turn, affects the first party's (A) reputation as a cooperator or noncooperator, and it is the threat of being gossiped about that keeps (A) from defecting. That is, it is the threat of being gossiped about that keeps people in line.
(3) Third parties (C), in turn, base their decision whether or not to cooperate with (A) based on this reputational information.

Hence, each of the three mechanisms needs to work if cooperation is to be sustained. The link between reputation and cooperation (step 3) constitutes the core of the triangle. If reputational information is available and correct, and the rules of the game allow selecting and abandoning exchange partners, cooperation can in principle be sustained. But as this section will show, the interrelations between them are less straightforward than they appear at first glance. First, reputations may be biased, incomplete, or wrong (Fehr & Sutter, 2019; Fonseca & Peters, 2018; Sommerfeld et al., 2008), which may severely undermine the alleged corrective effect of reputation on selecting the "right" exchange partners, as postulated in arrow 3 of Figure 1.

Second, experienced (non-)cooperation may not always lead to gossiping, as implied in arrow 1 of Figure 1. In fact, there are many good reasons why individuals may even deliberately refrain from sharing this information with others (Giardini & Wittek, 2019b). Conversely, gossip may be triggered by many other motives than the desire to share information about somebody's (non-)cooperative behavior. Third, gossiping may not always have reputational effects, as stipulated in arrow 2 of Figure 1. For example, as one study has demonstrated, much gossiping anticipates the potential approval by the receivers, thus mainly echoing the receiver's evaluation of the third party (Burt, 2001).

1.2.1 The Available Scientific Record on Gossip, Reputation, and Cooperation Reveals Major Empirical Inconsistencies

Empirically, a key puzzle in cooperation research is the consistently replicated finding that contributions to public-good experiments start at high to moderate levels, but then show a steady decline over time due to the proportion of "free riders" increasing. Or, as one scholar recently has succinctly summarized it: "The ability to cooperate is a central condition for human prosperity, yet a trend of declining cooperation is one of the most robust observations in behavioral economics" (Fosgaard, 2018, p. 1). This pattern has been documented by two influential reviews, published almost two decades apart (Chaudhuri, 2011; Ledyard, 1995). More recent studies show similar outcomes (Andreozzi et al., 2020; Burton-Chellew et al., 2015; Duca & Nax, 2018; Fosgaard, 2018). These patterns constitute a major challenge for the dominant narrative that considers reputation processes as the golden key to sustainable cooperation. Even more important, there are no empirical or field studies to date about how reputation sustains cooperation over time, and the available knowledge on the topic comes mostly from computational models.

Early attempts to explain this consistent decline of cooperation point, among others, to decision errors or argue that the players need some time until they have learned to play the dominant strategy (which is not to cooperate). More recent accounts seek the explanation for cooperation decay in the heterogeneity of player types or stable *dispositions*, distinguishing between conditional cooperators and free riders. Whereas conditional cooperators are optimistic concerning the contributions of others and therefore contribute, they discover through time that others free-ride, which in turns leads them to reduce their contributions. Hence the decay in cooperation. The conclusion from many experimental studies is that people who are conditional cooperators act like this independently of the situation they find themselves in. But, as other researchers have pointed out, the assumption of stable preferences, also for conditional cooperation, is quite a strong one. It cannot be ruled out that conditional cooperation, rather than being the result of a person's "type," may be the plain consequence of this person being responsive to group pressure, as Chaudhuri (2011) remarks in a footnote, referring to empirical findings from Bardsley and Sausgruber (2005) and Carpenter (2004). Conditional cooperation therefore may reflect adjustment to the social context – in this case conforming to the expectations of others (Dana et al., 2007; Heintz et al., 2015), rather than being the consequence of a stable preference for conditional cooperation.

Another puzzling insight related to the alleged stability of individual dispositions is that gossip may be motivated by what has been called the "dark triad," that is, "a constellation of personality traits, characterized by callousness and the tendency to manipulate others to one's own benefit": psychopathy, Machiavellianism, and narcissism (Kniffin & Wilson, 2005). If gossip is mainly spread by individuals with this kind of psychopathological trait, then questions arise about the viability of reputation as a reliable mechanism governing cooperation.

The internal *structure* of groups – such as the web of social and functional relationships linking its members – can be another potential factor leading to reputation mechanisms failing to sustain cooperation, because gossip does not work as predicted. Kniffin and Wilson (2005) stress that the incidence of gossiping is likely to be higher in settings with stronger interdependence and shared goals, as is frequently the case in work contexts. But there are also reasons to be cautious about this kind of claim. Regardless of the fact that most cultures have strong norms prohibiting gossip, and that most gossip research implicitly assumes that these norms are violated on a large scale, there are many situations in which it may *not* be in the best interest of a potential gossiper to share sensitive third-party information with others. This is illustrated by an interview study with 251 physicists and biologists in three different countries. Exploring the role of gossip as a means of social control related to scientific misconduct, the authors concluded that whereas gossip can be punitive, it is usually not corrective and therefore often not effective (Vaidyanathan et al., 2016). As the accounts from victims of scientific misconduct vividly describe, all of them think twice before bad mouthing another scientist, be it a colleague, a superior, and in particular high-status seniors. Too strong is the fear of potential repercussions for one's own career or reputation. The study also adds to earlier observations concerning the detrimental effects gossip may have on trust and morale (Akande & Odewale, 1994; Baker & Jones, 1996; Van Iterson & Clegg, 2008), and to field research that has put the purported ubiquity of gossip into perspective. For example, a study by Dunbar, Duncan, and Marriott (1997), based on systematic eavesdropping in trains, reports that "only about 3–4% of conversation time centers around 'malicious' (or negative) gossip in the colloquial sense" (p. 242). Unfortunately, there is hardly any systematic empirical research about the conditions under which potential gossip is quite likely *not* to be shared (Giardini & Wittek, 2019b).

Furthermore, also the characteristics of the "moment" or the *situation* may significantly impact the proper functioning of gossip-based reputation mechanisms. For example, whereas a straightforward approach to explain reactions to norm violations would suggest a linear correlation between the severity of the infraction (e.g., in terms of the negative effects for others) and the strength of the reaction, this is not always the case. According to this view, people would leave it at gossiping when faced with minor infractions, and resort to more direct confrontations for major ones (Ellickson, 1991). But the limited evidence that is available is not entirely consistent with this proportionality proposition. It suggests that gossip as a reaction to norm violations occupies a separate cognitive category, rather than being part of a single ladder of escalation. Instead, its use strongly depends on the characteristics of the situation, such as whether the offense represents a mishap or is part of a pattern that signals lack of normative commitment by the norm violator (Wittek, 2013). But this is further complicated by the fact that there seem to be *cultural* differences with regard to how appropriate gossiping is considered to be as a reaction to norm violations. For example, Eriksson et al. (2021) found that gossip is more likely to be seen as an appropriate reaction to norm violations in individualist rather than collectivist societies with higher power distance, whereas other studies claim exactly the opposite (Greif, 1994). In sum, the cognitive mechanisms related to situational and cultural variations introduce yet another set of sources of potential gossip failure.

1.2.2 The Theoretical Foundation of Gossip Research Is Incomplete and Fragmented

Research on the triangle of reputation, gossip, and cooperation also faces at least two theoretical challenges. The first challenge refers to its incompleteness and fragmentation. It has three aspects. First, one issue relates to the large variety of conditions that were identified as causally relevant at *multiple levels of analysis*. As outlined in the previous section, researchers have linked gossip, reputation, and cooperation to intercultural and institutional variations at the level of nations, geographical regions, small groups, and organizations; to differences in an individual's social position and personal social networks; to (new) means of communication, such as social media; to differences in personality traits and other individual-level dispositions; and to variations in specific social situations. Whereas empirical evidence leaves no doubt about the fact that each of these context conditions affects reputation, gossip, and cooperation, so far little effort has been made to analyze their interplay and relative impact.

Second, much theorizing covers only part of the triangle, and sometimes does not disentangle different elements. There are three different literatures involving cooperation in combination with either reputation, gossip, or both (see Figure 2). Only a relatively small fraction simultaneously addresses the overlap of all three (GRC in Figure 2). The bulk of the literature consists of research on the antecedents of gossip and its eventual consequences, but this is not necessarily related to cooperation. This is followed by models focusing either on reputation or on gossip as antecedents of cooperation. This incompleteness is further aggravated by the fact that studies on gossip, reputation, and cooperation usually address only parts of the "gossip triad" (Giardini & Wittek, 2019a), leaving many assumptions implicit. As our recent review has shown (Giardini & Wittek, 2019a), even the four major explanatory mechanisms (reciprocity, punishment, coalition, and control) each rely on different assumptions and

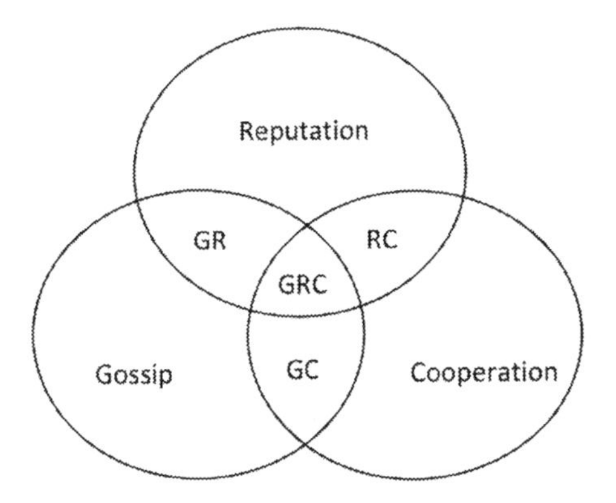

Figure 2 Venn diagram of research domains

focus on different actors. For example, indirect reciprocity explanations focus on reputation effects for gossip targets and senders to explain changes in cooperation sustainability involving the target and the sender, whereas coalition models stress the importance of reputation effects for all three actors in the triad and link them to changes in cooperation sustainability among them. But a convincing model needs to be able to provide a consistent explanation not only for what might instigate a potential gossip sender to share third-party information. The same principles that are used to model cognitions, motivations, and behavior of potential gossip senders should also be able to capture the cognitions, motives, and behavior of the other actors in the gossip triad. So far, current theorizing seems to be far from such an integrated perspective, instead recurring on a large variety of disconnected "psychological effects" (Manrique et al., 2021). For example, Martinescu et al. (2019) stress the importance of emotions as an antecedent and consequence of gossip for senders, receivers, and targets, whereas other researchers stress the social comparison motive for sender and receiver (Suls, 1977; Wert & Salovey, 2004), and still others point to aggression or prosociality as important motives to share gossip (Feinberg et al., 2012; Jeuken et al., 2015; Testori et al., 2022).

Competing assumptions about human nature pose a different theoretical problem. These range from game theoretical models explicitly building on assumptions of full strategic rationality and selfish gain seeking on the one hand, to explanations invoking a wide variety of "nonrational" motivations and cognitions related to humans' extraordinary capacity to cooperate (Bowles & Gintis, 2011; Nowak & Highfield, 2011) and the alleged innate prosociality of our species (Burton-Chellew & West, 2013; Burton-Chellew et al., 2015). The latter acknowledges that there may be systematic "deviations" from this model, which are also referred to as "cognitive biases" or "anomalies" (Camerer &

Thaler, 1995; Kahneman et al., 1991). Accordingly, individuals' motives to gossip have been attributed both to selfish and to group-serving intentions (Bertolotti & Magnani, 2014). But the question is not whether humans are either inherently prosocial or selfish, or which proportion of a group is of the "conditional cooperator" type, but rather under which conditions and why individuals keep acting cooperatively. The fact that different studies use different and often *incompatible behavioral microfoundations* makes theoretical integration difficult, if not impossible. Research meanwhile acknowledges the need for an integrated alternative microfoundation that is able to accommodate the seeming inconsistencies of earlier research (Haselton et al., 2015). We argue that goal framing theory, an evolutionary theory of behavioral microfoundations, offers the necessary tools for building an integrated theory of the relationship between gossip, reputation, and cooperation.

2 The Evolutionary Origins of Gossip, Reputation, and Cooperation

The evolution of human cooperation has been framed as a puzzle to solve (Boyd & Richerson, 2006), as a challenge (Apicella & Silk, 2019), and as a paradox (Nemeth & Takacs, 2010). In the last twenty years, a significant number of review papers in many different disciplines, from biology to statistical physics and from developmental psychology to anthropology (a query on Google Scholar for review papers on "evolution human cooperation" published between 2002 and 2022 reported 88,100 results), have tried to take stock of existing research and to provide a convincing answer to the question: "How did cooperative behavior evolve in self-interested humans?" Indirect reciprocity (Alexander, 1987; Santos et al., 2021) and partner choice (Roberts, 1998; Roberts et al., 2021) are regarded as the most convincing explanations of the evolution of cooperation among nonkin. The possibility of gaining a reputation for being cooperative is a common feature of these two theories, which imply that reputations result from the past behaviors of actors and that the evaluation of these actions has consequences that can promote and sustain cooperation. Indirect reciprocity has perhaps been the most influential model of reputation-based cooperation (Alexander, 1987; Nowak & Sigmund, 1998; Panchanathan & Boyd, 2004). In this framework, individuals decide to cooperate (or not) with another, and this is reflected in the "image score" of the individuals, which will affect whether third parties cooperate with them (or not) in a future encounter (Leimar & Hammerstein, 2001; Nowak & Sigmund, 1998). Even if costly in the short run, reputational benefits gained through cooperation largely repay the initial investment. The benefits of a positive reputation are even larger according to the theory of competitive altruism, in which cooperation is a strategy to stand out and be selected for profitable partnerships (Barclay, 2016; Barclay & Barker, 2020; Roberts et al., 2021). In such a "biological market" (Noë & Hammerstein, 1995) positive reputations can be even more valuable than in a setting based on indirect reciprocity where partners are randomly drawn from the population (Nowak & Sigmund, 1998). Before the formulation of the theory of indirect reciprocity (Alexander, 1987; Nowak & Sigmund, 1998, 2005) reputation and gossip were on the research agenda of anthropologists (Gluckman, 1968; Paine, 1968) and social scientists (Ben Ze'ev & Goodman, 1994; Emler, 1994; Goffman, 1949). The work of anthropologists, sociologists, and psychologists complements biological theories by providing an overview of the functions served by gossip that are presumably rooted in our ancestral past (Boehm, 2019; Dunbar, 1996; McAndrew, 2019).

The explanations offered by the theories of indirect reciprocity and competitive altruism are both extremely influential and compelling, but they also rest on a set of simplifying assumptions. Evidence collected in highly controlled laboratory settings and theoretical insights from analytical and computational models provide support for indirect reciprocity theory and partner choice. However, there is an increasing awareness that in human groups gossip can be used to circulate false or inaccurate information, thus resulting in reputations that, being inaccurate, can hardly support cooperative behaviors and their evolutions (Giardini et al., 2022).

The link between evolution, gossip, and cooperation has been thoroughly explored in recent years, based on the assumption that knowing other people's deeds before interacting with them can be a powerful tool to establish and support cooperation. In a complementary way, the consequences of being regarded as a defector in any kind of social interactions has such an array of negative consequences, that the "threat of gossip" is sufficient to enforce cooperation in multiple settings (for a review, see Giardini et al., 2021). Reputation is a belief or a meta-belief about what others think about someone (Giardini & Wittek, 2019a), and it can be the end result of different kinds of behaviors (observation of someone's actions, gossip, direct information from the target of reputation) performed by a multiplicity of actors. In what follows we will focus only on gossip intended as the action of spreading valuable information about an absent third party (Emler, 1994; Giardini & Wittek, 2019a). Gossip involves three specific relational acts: an act of attribution of some qualities, positive or negative, to someone else; an act of sharing, that is, communicating this attribution; and, finally, an act of perception by the receiver. Although the term "gossip" usually refers to what the sender does, the behavior is triadic in nature because there are three actors involved: the gossiper (or sender), the receiver, and the target (or object). When deciding whether, how, and to whom to gossip, these triadic relations enter the decision of the gossiper. The strength of the connections, together with the embeddedness of the gossip triad in a larger social network, all influence the occurrence and content of gossip, with possible effects on the reputation of the three actors, and on their cooperation (Giardini & Wittek, 2019a). The question is: what is the evolutionary basis of such a complex decision in humans?

2.1 Tinbergen's Four Questions

Theoretical biology has greatly contributed to our understanding of cooperation among unrelated individuals since the work of Charles Darwin, specifying the mechanisms and processes that have shaped the behaviors we observe today. In a similar manner, evolutionary psychology has devoted special attention to the evolution of gossip and reputation, with several studies suggesting that the evolution of gossip was tightly related with the enlargement of human groups and the appearance of several features of human sociality (Barkow, 1992; Dunbar, 1996; McAndrew, 2019).

In this section, we refer to the four questions designed by Niko Tinbergen (1963) to explain the evolutionary roots of animal behavior, and we use them as an analytical tool to structure our discussion about the evolution of gossip. Despite Tinbergen's emphasis on the need for answering all questions, all four questions have been addressed only with regard to few phenomena, and gossip, as a complex behavior, is no exception. The four questions are not limited to explaining animal behavior, but they apply broadly to any characteristic in living (and even some nonliving) systems (Bateson & Laland, 2013).

Tinbergen pointed out that there are four fundamentally different types of questions that need to be answered in order to fully comprehend a behavior. These four questions can be asked about any feature of an organism: (1) What is it for (its adaptive function)? (2) How did it develop during the lifetime of the individual (its ontogeny)? (3) How did it evolve over the history of the species (its phylogeny)? and (4) How does it work (what are the proximate mechanisms)? (Bateson & Laland, 2013). Each question helps define the key features of a certain behavior or trait, and their combination is expected to provide a full account of their evolutionary roots. These four levels of analysis are complementary, not mutually exclusive: all behaviors require an explanation at each of these four levels of analysis to be fully understood.

Function (or adaptive significance – Nesse, 2019 – or current utility – Bateson & Laland, 2013) refers to the evolutionary goal of a trait, defined by its effect on genetic fitness. Traits and behaviors are adaptive when their functions improve the fitness of an organism, thus making it more likely to survive and reproduce. Ontogeny refers to the process of development that makes it possible for an organism to have that trait, and phylogeny (or evolution) refers to the historical sequence whereby the trait was acquired within a biological lineage. Finally, mechanisms identify explanations at the cognitive, behavioral, or anatomical levels that make it possible for an organism to achieve this functional goal (Dunbar, 2009). These four levels of explanation are grouped according to the ultimate-proximate distinction (Mayr, 1963). Ultimate explanations refer to the fitness consequences of a trait or behavior and whether it is (or is not) selected. This class of explanations addresses evolutionary function (the "why" question), whereas proximate explanations relate to the way in which that functionality is achieved, that is, the "how" question (Scott-Phillips et al., 2011).

Gossiping, and the resulting reputations, allows humans to adapt and adjust to the complex social environments they inhabit (Emler, 2019). Different disciplines have contributed various perspectives on its evolutionary and developmental roots, functions, antecedents, consequences. The importance of gossip for the evolution of human sociality (Dunbar, 1996; 1996) and cooperation has received considerable attention (Barkow, 1992; Giardini & Wittek, 2019a; Milinski, 2019; Sommerfeld et al., 2007), and several theories have been put forward to explain how gossip evolved and how it might have contributed to the evolution of cooperation in our species. Here, we use Tinbergen's questions to understand how and why gossip might have evolved.

2.2 Tinbergen's Four Questions Applied to Gossip

2.2.1 What Is It For?

"What is it for?" has been asked time and again about gossip. Several functions have been attributed to gossip, but it is not always possible to distinguish between functions that are mostly beneficial for the individual and functions that are also beneficial for the group. Gossip evolved because it provided some direct or indirect fitness benefits in the form of information sharing, punishment, group cohesion, and bonding: acquiring info about defectors, punishing them without being retaliated against, and creating bonds with cooperators provide fitness advantages. The first function, information acquisition, is definitely crucial for the survival of the actor who gains the information, but the spreading of the same information can also benefit the group. "Cultural learning" (e.g., Baumeister et al., 2004) and "social learning" refer to learning ingroup norms or one's place in a group (e.g., Eckert, 1990; Fine & Rosnow, 1978; Gottman & Mettetal, 1986), thus reinforcing hierarchies and status differences. Knowing who is higher in status can be crucial for survival, because those higher in status are also more powerful; that is, they can mobilize resources to support or attack other group members. McAndrew, Bell, and Garcia (2007) argue that gossip functions as a status-enhancing mechanism, and they propose a multilevel selection perspective, meaning that a given trait, in this case the ability to gossip, evolved to fulfill both genetic and social group purposes.

Gossip allows one to acquire new and important knowledge about threats and opportunities (e.g., Watkins & Danzi, 1995) by promoting strategy learning (De Backer, 2005), which is a way to learn what can be dangerous and what can be rewarding or useful in a given environment. Knowing about others is crucial for social comparison (e.g., Wert & Salovey, 2004), which permits one to acquire in a relatively inexpensive way useful knowledge about whether someone is doing better or worse in the group, and behave accordingly. This form of social comparison is emotionally safer than being publicly compared to other people, and it is less impactful on one's social standing in case the comparison is negative for the actor. Assuming an intra-group competition perspective, gossip can be regarded as an evolved strategy to compete for valuable and scarce resources by spreading either positive information about oneself, or negative information about others. Using a variety of experimental methods, Hess and Hagen (2021) found that gossip content is specific to the context of the competition, and that allies deter negative gossip and increase expectations of reputational harm to an adversary. Their results also point out that more valuable and scarce resources cause gossip, particularly negative gossip, to intensify, a finding in accordance with previous research about strategic information spreading as a way to deflect the negative consequences of lying (Giardini et al., 2019). Not only has gossip been linked to within-group competition (Hess & Hagen, 2019), but it has been considered a specific competitive tool for intrasexual competition (Davis et al., 2019). Campbell (2004) argued that women primarily compete through advertising (by enhancing their appearance) and through competitor derogation by using gossip (Vaillancourt, 2013) to tarnish other women's reputations.

The second function of gossip, documented across many different kinds of groups and settings, is sanctioning, social control, or "policing" (e.g., Wilson et al., 2000). Gossip is usually regarded as a low-cost form of punishment (Giardini & Conte, 2012; Villatoro et al., 2011) that is less dangerous than physical confrontation and more effective than institutional sanctions. In contexts in which the sanctions are gradual, going from gossip to ostracism and to legal sanction (Ellickson, 2009; Greif, 1989), gossip represents the simplest and more frequent form of punishment that, through the threat to someone's reputation, can police norm violations. Not only in small, close-knit communities

(Boehm, 2019; Brenneis, 1984) but also in larger groups and organizations (Ellwardt et al., 2012; Wittek & Wielers, 1998; Yoeli et al., 2013), gossip functions to promote norm-abiding behavior and discourage deviance. Similarly, in groups facing forced integration, such as the Makah Indians, gossip's function was to maintain the unity, morals, and values of the groups by exposing those who violated group norms (e.g., Gluckman, 1963).

Third, gossip creates bonds among individuals. Dunbar (1996, 2004) proposed that gossip (and language more generally) evolved to facilitate social bonding and social cohesion in the remarkably large groups that characterize human primates. "Exploitation of more predator-risky habitats requires an increase in group size; to make this possible, it is necessary both to evolve the cognitive machinery to underpin the management of the social relationships involved (essentially a larger neocortex) and to invest more time in the necessary bonding processes" (Dunbar, 1996, p. 103).

2.2.2 How Does Gossip Develop during the Lifetime of the Individual?

The developmental trajectory of gossip (how did it develop during the lifetime of the individual?) has received less attention, with a few notable exceptions (Ingram, 2019). Gossip is a complex behavior that entails a set of different skills that develop at different times, depending on both brain- and motor-systems maturation and on exposure to social contacts. Ingram (2019) proposed a sequence of developmental stages for gossip, going from a very early sensorimotor stage (0–2 years), through intuitive and operational stages, until the display of full-fledged gossip behavior around fourteen years. The ontogeny of gossip is very much related to the development of language skills that tend to be fully in place between two and four years of age, together with the ability to report the behavior of other people (den Bak & Ross, 1996). Before that, children already possess a theory of mind that allows them to interpret others' actions as goal-directed and to report violations to third parties (Tomasello & Vaish, 2013). Other elements that are required for developing this behavior are norm internalization (Kochanska, 2002) and the ability to represent how one's behavior can be evaluated by others (Piazza et al., 2011). Five-year-old children are consistently more generous when they know they are being observed (Shaw et al., 2014), and this sensitivity to the presence of observers has been linked to heightened cooperation in several studies with adult participants (Manesi et al., 2016). Two recent studies have found that five-year-old children will provide prosocial gossip by informing on a selfish peer (Engelmann et al., 2016) and that by age seven, children believe that firsthand experience is more valuable than third-party gossip (Haux et al., 2017).

2.2.3 How Did Gossip Evolve over the History of the Species?

Asking "how did gossip evolve over the history of the species?" can be tentatively answered by looking into what gossip evolved out of, and how. Tinbergen framed this as understanding how natural selection had operated in the past, providing the genetic basis for what an individual inherits (Bateson & Laland, 2013). Theory of mind (Tomasello et al., 2012) was certainly a key player in making gossip possible, together with language abilities that coevolved with relative brain size (Dunbar, 1996). Attributing thoughts and goals to others, the ability cognitive scientists call "theory of mind" (Premack & Woodruff, 1978), is central to our social life. Thanks to theory of mind, humans are able to attribute thoughts, intentions, and desires to others, and use these attributions to predict, adjust to, or justify others' behaviors. A theory of mind is crucial to attribute intentions to the target's actions, but also to formulate expectations about the reactions of one or more receivers to what is reported. The same action, for instance failing to meet a deadline for a team project, can be interpreted as an intentional attempt to sabotage the group, as a lack of time management skills, or as an innocent mistake due to personal circumstances. The interpretation of this action and the projected consequences of gossip, however, can make it more or less worthy of transmitting. The benefits brought about by gossip in terms of social bonding can also be related to the changing circumstances in the history of the human species, such as, for instance, the enlargement of human groups. As Dunbar (2004, p. 103) explained:

> Humans represent the most extreme point in this sequence within the primates because hominid evolution has been characterized by the exploitation of increasingly open terrestrial habitats, both of these features being associated with increased predation risk. . . . Language became part of this story because, at some point in hominid evolutionary history, the group size required exceeded that which could be bonded through social grooming alone; the constraint in this context was the fact that the time investment required by grooming is ultimately limited by the demands of foraging. Language enabled hominids to break through that particular glass ceiling because it allows time to be used more effectively than is possible with grooming: Speech allows us both to interact with a number of individuals simultaneously (grooming is a strictly one-on-one activity) and to exchange information about the state of our social network (lacking language, monkeys and apes are limited in their knowledge of their network by what they themselves see).

2.2.4 What Are the Proximate Causes of Gossiping?

The last question refers to the proximate mechanisms underlying the behavior. Which triggers evoke gossiping? At the neurocognitive level, gossip is supported by three neural systems, and other systems can be activated for the recognition of stimuli and the implementation of decisions (Izuma, 2012; Tomasello et al., 2005). The three main networks are the reward system, the mentalizing network, and the self-control system (Boero, 2019). The ability to attribute intentions to others is crucial for forming evaluations, and this is complemented by the cognitive mechanisms for reward and self-control. Taken together, these mechanisms could provide evidence for the existence of specialized reputation-management abilities in humans. In order to be effective, these abilities need to be flexible and responsive to changing conditions and environments, thus requiring the involvement of several brain areas (Izuma, 2012; Knoch et al., 2009). Gossip has also been linked to the endocrine system, and a recent study shows that gossip increases oxytocin levels compared to emotional non-gossip conversation (Brondino et al., 2017).

Another key cognitive mechanism involved in gossip is epistemic vigilance (Mascaro & Sperber, 2009), which is the automatic tendency to care about and assess the validity of information obtained from other people. Emotions and affective states can also be considered among the proximate mechanisms of gossip behavior, given that it is fundamentally related to the well-being and adaptive success of all the individuals who are involved in gossip. Emotions play a crucial role in helping people navigate and interact with the physical, social, and cultural world (Keltner & Haidt, 1999), and negative (shame, guilt, contempt, anger) and positive (joy, enjoyment) emotions can equally contribute to explain how gossip works. In the next section we will introduce goal framing theory as a framework of the proximate mechanisms behind gossip and reputation.

3 A Goal Framing Perspective on Gossip, Reputation, and Cooperation

This section comes in three parts. We first sketch the diverging perspectives on human nature, disentangling their different views on psychological microfoundations. The second part provides a succinct summary of goal framing theory. This theory is rooted in earlier attempts to develop more accurate behavioral microfoundations (Kahnemann & Tversky, 2013; Lindenberg, 1981, 1985). It is best known for its application to problems of norm compliance (Keizer et al., 2008) and now increasingly used in a variety of research domains, such as organization science (Puranam, 2018), legal studies (Etienne, 2011), and research on environmental behavior. For a recent review of research using the approach see do Canto et al., 2023. Finally, we elaborate the link between goal framing theories microfoundational assumptions and the motives behind gossiping.

3.1 Coevolution of Rationality and Sociality

How gossip and reputation may affect the sustainability of cooperation crucially depends on the kind of assumptions one makes about human nature. Previous scholarship differs considerably with regard to these so-called microfoundations. Two general classes of microfoundations can be distinguished, depending on whether or not they incorporate the coevolution of rationality and sociality (Lindenberg, 2023).

Models building on assumptions of *strategic rationality* constitute the first class. They have in common that they assume that self-interested maximizing behavior is basic and can be used to explain how human sociality emerged (Cowden, 2012). Thus, basically rational choice and game theory (not rooted in evolutionary theory) are used to explain evolutionary processes (Leinfellner, 1998).

The second class of microfoundations is based on *social rationality*. Here it is assumed that human rationality and sociality coevolved. The most prominent approaches in this class come in three different versions, all focusing on a different aspect of evolutionary adaptation (Lindenberg, 2023). One emphasizes the importance of fast and frugal heuristics as a means to cope with complexity and uncertainty in the social and nonsocial environment (Gigerenzer & Gaissmaier, 2011; Goldstein & Gigerenzer, 2002). Adaptation consisted not in improving the ability to carry out complex calculations based on expected probabilities, as in the theoretical axioms of strategic rationality, but in being able to react quickly in different circumstances. This can be achieved by developing and following rules of thumb, such as imitating the successful, or cooperating if the partner cooperates. A second version of social rationality focuses on preferences. It argues that in addition to self-centered preferences, human rationality adapted to the need for cooperation with nonkin, which resulted in the development of social rationality that interprets the public social sphere as an arena in which participants play games with social preferences (*Homo ludens*, Gintis 2016). The foundation of the third version of social rationality is what has been called the "third speed of change" (Lindenberg, 2015): humans' situational adaptive capacity consisting in the flexible activation of mental constructs, such as goals, preferences, and heuristics (Lindenberg, 2023). This version of social rationality emphasizes *flexible activation*: mental constructs, goals, and motivations can change quickly, depending on the situation and the related differences and changes in the social and nonsocial environment. The changeability of the social environment requires the ability to flexibly (de)activate goals, depending on the situation. Lindenberg locates the roots of humans' sensitivity to situationally shifting saliences in the need for dyadic co-regulation. The latter is crucial for a wide range of situations, from sharing to mutual perspective taking, joint intentionality, and collaborative learning. In the course of evolution, the adaptive advantage of dyadic co-regulation and the related capacities to put ourselves into the shoes of others facilitated the ability to co-regulate with the group as a whole and with our future self. These capacities form the basis for experiencing group membership and the related normative goal frame, as well as concern for our resources in the future and the related gain goals.

Though the three approaches to social rationality emphasize different aspects of the coevolution of sociality and rationality, they are interrelated, in that mental concepts, and thus also the use of heuristics and social preferences, need to be activated in order to become relevant as motives and cognitions guiding behavior. Integrating the three versions of social rationality approaches, *goal framing theory* (GFT) provides the necessary analytical tools for explaining how gossip promotes cooperation.

3.2 Goal Framing Theory

Goal framing theory can be summarized by six interrelated key assumptions (Keizer et al., 2008; Lindenberg & Steg, 2007). First, at any point in time, human cognition is dominated by a single overarching mindset. "Dominant" means that the related mindset is salient. It is in the cognitive foreground and therefore "sets the mind" by structuring the related lower-level cognitions and motivations. Overarching mindsets are also called "goal frames." They have far-reaching consequences for what individuals pay attention to, what they value or find important, the kind of knowledge they draw on, and how they interpret a situation (Lindenberg, 2015, p. 150; Lindenberg & Foss, 2011).

Second, as triggers for human behavior, three types of overarching mindsets are most important: the hedonic, the gain, and the normative goal frame. The *hedonic goal frame* focuses on immediate satisfaction of basic needs, on feeling good right now. It is about seeking pleasure, excitement, self-esteem, and avoiding unpleasant feelings, thoughts, or events. Individuals in a hedonic goal frame focus on the present and in this sense are "myopic." They also pay less attention to the context, such as meeting the expectations of others or acting according to some norm.

In the *gain goal frame* humans focus on improving or guarding their resources. The gain goal frame is about anticipating one's future condition and therefore also implies a longer-term orientation and planning. It comes with investments and strategic behavior. When in a gain goal frame, individuals are more sensitive to changes in their resources than about how a situation feels or which kinds of behaviors would be approved or disapproved.

In the *normative goal frame*, the overarching mindset is "doing the right thing." This refers to acting appropriately with regard to the specific norms of a collectivity in a given situation. The normative goal frame defines a group-oriented overarching mindset, and it is the basis for the production of collective goods. Individuals will be attentive to what they think others expect them to do. A salient normative goal frame makes individuals less sensitive to changes in personal resources or how one feels right now.

Third, as a result of the development of co-regulation during human evolution, the a priori strengths of these three goal frames differ, with the hedonic goal frame being the strongest, followed by the gain goal frame and the normative goal frame.

Fourth, the three goal frames influence each other: whenever one of them is in the cognitive foreground, the others are in the cognitive background. Individuals' actions rarely are *entirely* guided by hedonic, gain, or normative concerns. When background goals are aligned with the content of the foreground goal, they may reinforce its salience. For example, as research on organizational cultures shows, work settings may be designed such that realizing profit for one's company is strongly connected to a strong professional work ethos, a sense of commitment to one's team, and the pleasures coming from a supportive corporate environment (Michel, 2011). When the background goals are in conflict with the foreground goal, they will temper the latter's salience. For example, normative concerns may keep the temptation to realize opportunistic gain seeking at bay even in business situations where this would be possible (Uzzi, 1996). When (one of) the background goals become so strong that it displaces the foreground goal, a frame switch is the result, with the previous foreground goal becoming a background goal itself.

Fifth, the combination of the a priori hierarchy in the strength of goal frames on the one hand, and the fact that background goals keep influencing the salience of the goal frame either by reinforcing or by tempering it has far-reaching implications. The normative goal frame, which is pivotal for sustaining cooperation, is constantly challenged by gain and hedonic background goals, making the normative goal frame inherently more brittle than the other two goal frames. It is important to realize that though inherently stronger than the normative goal frame, the gain goal frame is also subject to be sidelined by the hedonic goal frame. Hence, unless otherwise supported and constantly reinforced either by the other two goal frames, or by the social and nonsocial environments, both the gain goal and the normative goal frame will eventually decay and fade, giving way to the hedonic goal frame.

Finally, the social and nonsocial situational context – such as cultural practices, institutional arrangements, or social influence – has a strong impact on which goal frame is made salient, and which ones are relegated to or remain in the cognitive background. Goal framing theory assumes that such situational factors can overrule the influence of values (Steg et al., 2016) and personality (Chatman & Barsade, 1995).

In sum, GFT provides an evolutionarily grounded microfoundation that integrates the three different perspectives on social rationality that were developed as an alternative and correction to the shortcomings of models of strategic rationality. GFT not only reconciles the different claims about human nature (*Homo economicus* vs. *Homo socialis*), but also is among the very few frameworks that puts the fragility of cooperation center stage. These qualities make it particularly suitable for re-assessing the complex links between reputation, gossip, and cooperation.

3.3 A Goal Framing Perspective on Gossip

Much has been written about the causes and processes of gossip and reputation and its consequences for the sustainability of cooperation (Beersma & Van Kleef, 2012; Garfield et al., 2021; Giardini & Wittek, 2019a; Giardini et al., 2022; Manrique et al., 2021; Michelson & Mouly, 2004). This research has linked gossiping to a variety of individual motives, ranging from prosocial to antisocial, as well as to all kinds of different group outcomes, ranging from cohesion enhancing to the undermining of collective efforts. The present section uses GFT to reassess this research and to develop an integrative model of the interplay between gossip, reputation, and cooperation (Giardini & Wittek, 2019a, 2019b).

Building on GFT's assumption about the a priori hierarchy of goal frame saliences (hedonic > gain > normative), we argue that gossip is most likely performed in a hedonic goal frame. Gossip in a gain goal frame is less likely, and gossip in a normative goal frame is even less likely. It takes special conditions to evoke gossip in a gain goal frame, and more so when a normative goal frame is salient. For example, normatively motivated gossip may be a move of last resort, which will be used only if one has reason to doubt the norm violators' sustained commitment to comply with the group's professional and informal normative expectations.

The remainder of this section therefore explores the conditions under which gossip is hedonically motivated. This will be followed by a discussion of the special conditions under which gossip is not motivated by a salient hedonic goal frame, but by a gain or a normative goal frame.

3.3.1 The Hedonic Roots of Gossiping

Despite the surge of academic interest in gossip, systematic research into which motives trigger individual gossip behavior and "whether people gossip for different reasons in different situations" (Beersma & Van Kleef, 2012, p. 2643) is still scarce. Beersma and Van Kleef's (2012) comprehensive empirical study on gossip motives distinguishes four types of motives: to enjoy, to inform/validate, to influence others negatively, and to maintain group norms. These four motives clearly relate to the three overarching goal frames. First, enjoyment triggers stimulation and therefore contributes to the realization of a hedonic goal frame. Gathering information, according to Beersma and Van Kleef, is mainly related to validating one's own view. Being validated in what you think about others (in evaluative terms) feels good because it satisfies a fundamental need. Thus, both the enjoyment and the information motive are rooted in a salient hedonic goal frame. Third, Beersma and Van Kleef (2012) identify negative influence as self-serving, which corresponds to a salient gain goal frame. But note that the desire to exert negative influence could also be driven by a hedonic goal frame, as saying negative things about a third party may enhance one's feeling of superiority. Finally, the fourth motive they identify, group protection, is a normative goal.

Based on a study among 221 undergraduates at the University of Amsterdam who filled in the 22-item Motives to Gossip Questionnaire, Beersma and Van Kleef (2012) found that the four gossip motives differed significantly in terms of their perceived importance. The most important motives were validation and information gathering, followed by enjoyment. No significant difference was found between group protection and (self-serving) negative influence. These findings suggest that hedonic goals may indeed be a more important driver of gossip than gain or normative motives, as suggested by GFT. To assess to what degree the strength of the motives varies across situations, the same sample of 221 students was randomly divided into four groups, with each group being asked to read a different scenario. The scenarios differed along two dimensions: (a) whether a colleague's behavior violated or did not violate a workgroup helping norm, and (b) whether the receiver of the gossip was a colleague or a friend who didn't work at the organization. Validation/information gathering was the only motive that, for all four scenarios, significantly correlated with the self-reported tendency to instigate gossip. In the condition where the receiver is a colleague, and the behavior of the other colleague was a norm violation, negative influence and group protection showed significant, though much weaker, correlations with the tendency to gossip. This suggests that the salient hedonic motive behind gossip about norm violations by other ingroup members is flanked by weaker gain and normative concerns in the cognitive background. Taken together, the patterns revealed by Beersma and Van Kleef's study provide some circumstantial evidence for hedonic motives being one of the main proximate causes of gossiping, at least in the contemporary setting of a class of University undergraduates. Using Beersma and Van Kleef's (2012) scale, Hartung et al. (2019) also found evidence for the importance of validation and information gathering. They reported that "gossiping just for fun" is as important as a motive as relationship building and protecting others from harm. They also found that social enjoyment as a self-declared motive was more important in private than in work-related situations.

The next question then becomes: what are the evolutionary roots of the link between hedonic motives and gossip? Probably the most influential argument in this context was proposed by Dunbar (1997), who claimed that gossip in humans is what grooming is to nonhuman primates: it builds and sustains bonds with other group members (see Section 2). These alliances may turn out to be useful as potential future sources for support or resources, but also to prevent or mitigate future threats from others. The extensive dedication to grooming – research suggests that it depends on group size and species, and can take up to 17 percent of nonhuman primates' time – is sustained by the fact that grooming is "extremely effective at releasing endorphins. The flood of opiates triggered by being groomed (and perhaps even by the act of grooming itself) generates a sense of relaxation (grooming lowers the heart rate, reduces signs of nervousness such as scratching)" (Dunbar, 2004, p. 101). The evidence on human gossiping reveals many similarities, suggesting that humans experience participation in gossip episodes as a sender or receiver as an intrinsically gratifying activity that satisfies many individual needs. This includes stimulation, self-confidence, and personal bonding (Foster, 2004). Gossip is "fun," triggers a "warm glow" in the participants (Stirling, 1956), contributes to immediate satisfaction of needs for confirmation, bonding, belonging, and is closely tied to a wide range of emotions (Martinescu et al., 2019; Waddington & Fletcher, 2005).

Unfortunately, empirical evidence on the psychoneuroendocrinological correlates of gossiping is still scarce. However, a recent study on the hormonal responses of receiving gossip showed an increase in oxytocin – which, together with the neurotransmitters endorphin, dopamine, and serotonin, is one of the triggers of feelings of happiness. This increase was unrelated to psychological characteristics of the receiver, such as empathy, autistic traits, perceived stress, or envy (Brondino et al., 2017). In a complementary way, a series of experimental studies found that observing antisocial acts triggers negative affect, that sharing this information with others can reduce this negative affect, and that the reduction of negative affect is strongest for individuals with a prosocial orientation (Feinberg et al., 2012).

There is some evidence that culture-gene coevolution plays a key role in the observed interplay between gossip and negative affect, in particular its correlation with serotonin levels (Chiao & Blizinsky, 2010). This argument is based on the observation that one region in the serotonin transporter gene allows for two different expressions (the short S and the long L allele). The S allele was found to be associated with increased negative emotion (e.g., heightened anxiety, attentional bias to negative information) and increased risk for depression. Environmental risk factors that are known to trigger these outcomes are exposure to chronic life stress, in particular interpersonal conflict and loss or threat (Chiao & Blizinsky, 2010, p. 530). Population genetic studies show that the proportion of individuals carrying the S allele is geographically clustered in regions where collectivistic cultures prevail. For example, 70–80 percent of individuals in East Asian samples carry it, compared to 40–45 percent of individuals in European samples (Chiao & Blizinsky, 2010). Given the many negative mental health effects that may result from carrying the S allele in case of exposure to adverse social or environmental circumstances, one would expect the incidence of these disorders to be much higher in these regions (Chiao & Blizinsky, 2010). But the opposite is the case: the incidence of negative affect, such as anxiety and major depressive disorders, is far lower in East Asia than in Western populations. This is where gene-culture coevolution comes in: with its emphasis on social harmony, collectivistic cultural beliefs and values may fulfill an important "anti-psychopathology" function in that they reduce or temper exposure to chronic life stress, thereby neutralizing one of the major environmental risk factors triggering psychopathologies in genetically susceptible individuals. Also, cultural tightness (meaning strict norms and punishment for deviance) correlates with susceptibility to ecological threat and the short S allele in the serotonin neurotransmitter gene (Mrazek et al., 2013). Hence, collectivistic as well as "tight" cultural beliefs coevolved with the specific genetic disposition toward increased negative emotions (the "anti-psychopathology" function). This pattern is important for a model of gossip, because according to a standard account in the literature, members of collectivist cultures are considered to be more strongly inclined to gossip than members of individualist cultures.

In sum, if gossiping indeed has the power to temper negative affect, engaging in it is likely to foster the realization of hedonic goals. This has several implications. It means that the inclination to *initiate* a gossip episode will be stronger in situations where the hedonic goal frame is in the cognitive foreground. It also suggests that *participating* in a gossip episode may increase the salience of the receiver's hedonic goal frame. That is, gossiping helps to fulfill the sender's and receiver's desire to "feel better right now." Finally, if most of the time gossip is mainly driven by the fundamental need for validation and enjoyment for the sender and the receiver, its effects on third-party reputations may be much weaker than most current theorizing assumes. Combined with the ease with which third-party information can be shared, humans may indeed – as implied by most research – be predisposed to gossip wherever, whenever, and with whomever they can. But often, the reputation effects may be limited, as much of the information shared by a sender may not be new to the receiver and merely reinforce previously held opinions. As a consequence, in such situations, receiving gossip may not fundamentally change the receiver's behavior toward the third party.

In this plain form, the argument of the hedonic roots of gossiping remains too simplistic: we know that there are many situations in which gossip *does* have strong reputational effects. The question therefore is whether there are conditions under which a salient hedonic goal frame may nevertheless trigger such effects, or when gossip is governed by a gain or normative goal frame.

For one, whereas the immediate experience of being engaged in a specific gossip episode may be pleasurable, the perception that the tendency to gossip is endemic in one's specific immediate social environment may rather raise the salience of both gain and normative concerns. Knowing that gossip is frequent means that oneself is also likely to become a gossip target. The damages that this can cause may increase the salience of the normative goal frame.

Furthermore, even in populations of nonhuman primates, who grooms whom strongly depends on the group context and situational conditions. For example, analyzing 1,529 grooming partner choices in wild populations of sooty mangabeys and western chimpanzees, a recent study found a bias toward choosing groomee's with a higher rank in the social status hierarchy and a tendency not to groom those who had strong relationships with bystanders (Mielke et al., 2018). Earlier studies have shown that grooming time increases with group size but decreases with the proportion of females in the group (Lehmann et al., 2007). But whereas studies on nonhuman primates also seek to explain under which contextual and situational conditions grooming is far less frequent than expected, studies on gossiping so far have not engaged in such attempts. The result is that the field is strongly biased toward the presence of gossip (Dores Cruz et al., 2021), leaving us with very little insights about the situations in which individuals have sensible "gossip worthy" third-party information but refrain from sharing it with others (Giardini & Wittek, 2019b). From an evolutionary perspective, the capacity to assess under which conditions it is better not to share gossip, and thereby also to suppress the urge to give in to its hedonic pleasures, can have equally important adaptive value as transmitting such information in other circumstances might have. The gossip decision therefore needs to be analyzed in the context of the capacities for co-regulation with the group and the related normative goal frame, as well as one's future self and the related gain goal frame.

3.3.2 Gossip and the Gain Goal Frame

From a GFT perspective, the standard model linking gossip to cooperation sustainability is rooted in an incomplete behavioral microfoundation. It assumes selfish, strategically rational actors, for whom sharing reputational information for the sake of norm enforcement may pay off. A nice example of this perspective is Coleman's (1990) two-step model of norm enforcement. In this model, gain-seeking rational individuals use gossip as an almost costless means to find out about norm violators. These information exchanges also establish consensus about the kind and severity of the norm violation, and they provide insight into how strongly others condemn this behavior. According to Coleman (1990), this first step of information sharing would then facilitate solving the second-order free rider dilemma, that is, the tendency to let others do the sanctioning. Put differently, knowing that the group condemns the behavior of a norm violator, some group members may be willing to engage in sanctioning behavior. This usually comes with some cost, such as the discomfort and effort of having to directly confront somebody about their misdeeds. Hence, in these gossip models, gain seeking is still the primary motive or salient mindset behind norm enforcement through gossiping.

The incompleteness of the microfoundation is due to the one-sided focus on the gain goal frame and the related neglect of both the hedonic and the normative goal frame. Part of this limitation is built into the standard experimental paradigms that are used to study cooperation, which are based on incentives. For example, instructions given to subjects participating in public good experiments state that participants can earn money based on the choices they make during the game. By making the aspect of a market transaction and monetary reward salient, the experimenters set up a situation that primes a gain goal frame in the participants.

Gossip has been linked to a variety of gain goals. According to a theoretical model on gossip in organizations (Kurland & Pelled, 2000), gaining or maintaining different types of power is a prominent motive for gossiping. Building on the influential distinction between reward, coercive, expert, and referent power (French et al., 1959), Kurland and Pelled (2000) developed propositions about the differential impact of positive and negative gossip on these four forms of power. Important context conditions that are assumed to moderate these effects are the credibility and work-relatedness of gossip, and context factors such as relationship quality and organizational culture.

Lee and Barnes (2021) provide an elaborate microfoundation of gossip in the organizational context. Their model is based on the distinction between four types of gossip, depending on whether gossip is work or nonwork-related, and whether it is negative or positive. They refer to work-related negative vs. positive gossip as protection based vs. endorsement-based gossip, respectively. Nonwork-related negative vs. positive gossip is labeled derogation-based vs. communion-based gossip. Protection-based gossip serves the group, for example, by warning others about the unreliability of a coworker, which might have negative repercussions for the work or for those who engage with this colleague, and thereby directly or indirectly also might have detrimental consequences for the organization or the subunit as a whole. But endorsement-based gossip also has instrumental value. Praising a coworker's professional qualities and work-related behavior not only improves the reputation of the target and defines a positive reference point for evaluating one's own work, it also conveys knowledge about someone's expertise and competence. Such knowledge, in turn, can form an important source of social capital.

Lee and Barnes's model is insightful because it explicates the receiver's attribution of gossip sender's motives as a crucial mediator leading to behavioral responses by the receiver. Depending on the type of gossip, the receiver can perceive the sender as pursuing prosocial, relational, or self-interested motives related to the specific gossip event. By shifting the attention to the situation and the psychology of the receiver, this model transcends the standard model that uses behavioral types or dispositions: attributions of motives for the same sender can vary across different gossip episodes. The kind of attribution will then affect which of three types of reactions the receiver will engage in. At the level of the gossip episode, attributions of relational and prosocial motives increase the likelihood that the receiver will reciprocate the gossip, whereas the attribution of self-interested motives will decrease it. At the level of the individual sender, receivers' reactions can take the form of cooperation or social undermining, depending on whether the gossip enhances or compromises the sender's trustworthiness.

If the context is described as a network of relationship among the involved actors, the gain goal frame is assumed to be the primary motive guiding "brokerage" behavior of individuals occupying strategically central positions in social networks, that is, positions that span structural holes between otherwise unconnected contacts (Burt & Soda, 2021). Occupying such a position can yield a variety of benefits, as they may follow from different "brokering" activities. For example, the broker may be able to secure some advantages by playing one's contacts out against each other (the "tertius gaudens" strategy). Conversely, the broker may also benefit from facilitating exchanges between previously unconnected players (the "tertius iungens" strategy). More generally, spanning structural holes allows extracting a variety of control and information benefits, and gossiping is the main instrument to achieve this.

3.3.3 Gossip and the Normative Goal Frame

Normative concerns have been linked to gossiping since the topic has captured the interest of social scientists. An influential view sees gossip as the primary means to convey information about social norms and behavioral expectations, usually by derogating those who violated them (Baumeister et al., 2004; Merry, 1984). Among the various primary gossip motives that have been identified (Beersma & Van Kleef, 2012), group protection and prosocial gossip play a key role in enforcing norms (Feinberg et al., 2012; Testori et al., 2022). Seen from a goal framing perspective, the literature on gossip motives remains somewhat ambivalent on the role of normative obligations as the primary motive instigating a gossipmonger's move to share third-party information.

Invoking norms as a potential explanation for prosocial behavior implies that individuals do what they do because they feel that this is the right thing to do. This is usually strengthened by the belief that the members of their society or group consider the related behavior as the "normatively correct" one in a given situation (Bicchieri, 2017; House et al., 2020). If this normative goal frame is salient it may either trigger or temper the tendency to gossip. Moral outrage about antisocial behavior indeed has often been found to be a trigger of gossiping (Boehm, 2019), suggesting a salient normative mindset as the cognitive-motivational basis. But solidarity norms and the related salience of the normative goal frame may also inhibit the inclination to gossip, for example, in situations in which the potential gossip sender and the object have a strong personal bond. In such cases, strong solidarity norms that usually govern affective interdependence are likely to temper the inclination to gossip, even in the face of some norm violation: you do not talk behind the backs of your closest friends, even if this might yield you some benefit or because it might be fun (Giardini & Wittek, 2019b). Relatedly, network closure may strengthen the tendency to follow conversational conventions resulting in echoing redundant third-party information rather than sharing new, potentially damaging gossip (Burt, 2001). As in-depth studies of how gossip episodes unfold indeed show, before disclosing the sensitive content, potential gossip senders first "test the terrain" with regard to a potential receiver's receptivity for such evaluative information, and they proceed only if the receiver signals openness to it (Eder & Enke, 1991).

Finally, as outlined in our discussion of the model introduced by Lee and Barnes (2021), it is not only potential senders' salient goal frames that matter to explain under which conditions gossip will or will not be shared. Also, the receiver's mindset plays an important role: receivers' reactions will be cooperative if they believe the senders' gossiping aligns with norms of trustworthiness. Put differently: gossip's reputation effects on cooperation will be strongest in situations where the normative goal frame is salient for all three parties of the gossip triad.

4 Gossip: Antecedents and Consequences for Reputation and Cooperation

According to a widely shared perspective, reputation-based gossip provided a key social mechanism to sustain cooperation during large parts of human evolution, and it did so most effectively in small group settings (Dunbar, 1997). In the course of the centuries, this societal context has morphed into a complex, technology-dependent, and globally networked environment. From an evolutionary point of view, this raises the question whether – and if so, to what degree and how – a mechanism that had evolved primarily as a social process regulating interactions between natural persons within bounded small-scale social communities still plays a meaningful role in sustaining cooperation in complex societies. If we follow the "standard model" of gossip and reputation, the simplicity and robustness of the related mechanisms should also be highly effective to sustain cooperation in contemporary society.

However, gossip's capacity to have reputation effects crucially depends on the normative goal frame being salient for those involved. This requires that the strong a priori dominance of the hedonic and gain goal frames is tempered or aligned with the normative goal frame. The present section discusses four types of conditions that affect the salience of specific goal frames and therefore have important repercussions on the prevalence of gossip and its ability to foster cooperation: cultural beliefs, social structure, individual-level dispositions, and situational conditions.

4.1 Cultures

Culture, or shared meaning, permeates any aspect of human society. The related beliefs and expectations not only have a strong influence on how we expect others to behave in different situations, but they also contribute to creating shared norms and institutions (Heine, 2010). They also have been invoked to explain societal and group- or organization-level variations in the prevalence of gossip and its beneficial or detrimental outcomes for groups and individuals. In this section we investigate the specific cultural beliefs – both at the level of society as a whole and at the level of organizations – under which a salient normative goal frame may or may not lead to gossip and the related reputation effects. Three types of cultural beliefs will be investigated in more detail: collectivism vs. individualism, high vs. low trust, and strong vs. weak gossip cultures.

4.1.1 Collectivist Cultures

The notion of a collectivist culture refers to a coherent set of beliefs stressing the importance of the ingroup and interdependence. Collectivists prioritize the goals of their ingroup over their personal goals, whereas individualists value autonomy and independence (Triandis, 2001). Though traces of both collectivism and individualism can be found in every culture, and adherence to the respective values and beliefs is a matter of degree and individual differences, overall tendencies toward one cultural belief system or the other can be detected at the aggregate level of populations. According to GFT, both collectivist and individualist cultures influence a priori goal frame salience, but each comes with different types of normative expectations. As a result, a straightforward direct effect of the collectivism-individualism dimension on gossip is unlikely. Yet, the claim that gossip is more likely in societies with collectivist, rather than individualist, cultural beliefs and that it fosters ingroup cooperation at the expense of cooperation with outgroups is probably the most influential claim linking culture to the tendency to share third-party information (Greif, 1994). The historical evidence supporting this claim was based on a comparison of the business practices of the collectivist Maghribi and the individualist Genovese long-distance traders of the eleventh and twelfth centuries. Merchants in both communities faced the identical business challenge to find trustworthy agents who would reliably handle their merchandise abroad. But the two communities clearly differed on the collectivist-individualist dimension. One of the traits distinguishing the two cultural belief systems is the expectation to share third-party information with others in the community and to invest in collective punishment. This tendency is assumed to be strong in collectivist cultures, and indeed was a feature of the culture of Maghribi traders: each of them exchanged letters with a large number of other Maghribi traders, relating their own and others' experiences with agents. The opposite was the case for their Genovese counterparts, who had a reputation for their strong individualist orientation, which translated, among others, in being "jealous of their business secrets."

Because they could rely on the gossip about trustworthy and untrustworthy agents shared by other merchants in their letters, Maghribi would hire exclusively agents from the Maghribi community. In contrast, lacking such a reliable source of information, Genovese would also hire non-Genovese as agents, for example, the traders native to the area of destination. With cooperative business transactions in collectivistic cultures being restricted to their own community, segregated patterns are the result. In contrast, individualist cultures favor integration across different economic and social communities, but lack the self-enforcing powers of collective punishment that forms the core of collectivistic communities. In sum, if we follow Greif's argument, individualist beliefs and the related relative lack of a culture of gossiping may have laid the foundation for sustained intergroup cooperation, whereas collectivist beliefs and their emphasis on information sharing sustained ingroup cooperation but at the expense of cooperation with outgroups.

Greif's claim is based on an investigation of a very specific case, two different Medieval communities of long-distance traders, who had to solve a very specific principal–agent problem. The question is whether the postulated causal chain between culture (collectivism vs. individualism), gossip, and sustained in- vs. outgroup cooperation indeed can also be generalized to contemporary society and to a broader range of settings such as communities and organizations (Huff & Kelley, 2003). It is evident that a straightforward generalization of this specific historical case to other contexts is problematic, not at least because the kind of "gossip" involved actually consists of written exchange of business information. This makes the social context markedly different from the face-to-face exchange of third-party information that usually characterizes gossip episodes.

In fact, the handful of studies exploring at least parts of this equation cast doubt on this claim. In line with GFT, the discovered patterns suggest that the underlying mechanisms are less straightforward than the original hypothesis proposed. Goal framing theory suggests that embeddedness in a specific cultural belief system raises the a priori salience of the specific goal frames this cultural system prioritizes. For example, a collectivist belief system attaches higher value on *sacrificing personal goals for the benefit of one's ingroup*, raising the salience of ingroup support norms and decreasing the salience of the personal gain motive. But GFT also suggests that since situational variations strongly contribute to shifting the salience of goal frames, it is key to analyze the interplay between the cultural context and the degree to which individuals follow it on the one hand, and situation-specific cues on the other hand. Situational cues, if strong enough, may push the salient cultural mindset into the cognitive background. Goal framing theory predicts that direct effects of general cultural beliefs on gossip and cooperation are likely to be weak at best, and that the strength of their effect depends on whether the specific situational cues are aligned or at odds with the goal frames prioritized by the cultural belief system (see also the discussion on situations later in this section). One specific GFT prediction along this line is that for individuals holding collectivist beliefs, strong situational hedonic cues can increase an individual's tendency to gossip in two ways. First, they can push normative concerns that would normally inhibit negative talk about one's ingroup members into the cognitive background, thereby also triggering gossip about ingroup members. Second, they may exacerbate negative feelings toward outgroups, thereby fostering gossip about outgroup members.

The strong effect of hedonic situational cues on gossiping indeed becomes evident in an empirical study investigating how the interplay between individual collectivist beliefs and organizational stressors such as time stress affect employees' inclination to engage in gossip about colleagues and the repercussions this has for individual performance (De Clercq et al., 2019). Statistical analysis of data from a longitudinal survey among 198 members (10 percent of whom were women) of 10 organizations in Pakistan showed that gossiping as a reaction to perceived time stress was significantly more likely for individuals holding strong collectivist beliefs than for employees holding individualist beliefs (De Clercq et al., 2019). Furthermore, gossip was found to mediate the negative impact of time stress on supervisor-rated job performance because it consumes precious working time. As predicted by GFT, the urge to vent one's frustrations about work stress by gossiping reflects the process in which a grievance provides a situational cue that pushes the hedonic goal frame into the cognitive foreground. The felt desire to derogate colleagues whose shortcomings allegedly contribute to work stress is exacerbated by the normative expectations that come with a collectivistic orientation: "We argue, then, that employees with a strong collectivistic orientation might enjoy spreading negative rumors about others in the organization when they suffer from time-related work stress, because doing so appears to be an acceptable, desirable response" (De Clercq et al., 2019, p. 6). According to the authors of the study, given collectivism's emphasis on the primacy of the ingroup, gossip targets are likely to be colleagues outside the direct inner circle of one's immediate work environment, an assumption their study could not test.

Overall, as our analyses of selected studies revealed, there is little evidence that the influential *collectivism breeds gossip* hypothesis also holds in contemporary settings. The strength of a cultural belief system does affect gossip and cooperation, but as predicted by GFT, its effects strongly depend on situational differences.

4.1.2 Trust Cultures

Shared cultural beliefs about the trustworthiness of others are a second important dimension affecting gossiping and cooperation. GFT predicts that the salience of trust and fairness norms temper the gain and hedonic mindsets that otherwise might undermine intelligent effort and cooperation. This argument also is in line with earlier research showing the importance of organizational cultures in general, and of high-trust vs. low-trust organizational cultures in particular.

Focusing on the link between gossip and cultural beliefs at the level of (work groups in) modern formal organizations, Kniffin and Wilson (2010) proposed what can be described as a *dual contingency gossip hypothesis*. Using an evolutionary multilevel selection framework and comparing available qualitative evidence from a ranching community, a rowing team, and work teams in an airport unit of a multinational airline, they argued that gossip indeed can have similar group-serving consequences, but only if two conditions are met: rewards need to be distributed on the basis of group-level performance, and the related rules and conventions governing the distribution of rewards need to be perceived as fair. In such settings, group members have an interest to mutually monitor each other and to share gossip about those whose actions hurt joint production.

Another study (De Clercq, 2022) reveals that "high-trust" organizational cultures inhibit gossiping as a reaction on norm violations. Organizational settings that are perceived as high-trust cultures temper the salience of the hedonic goal frame and strengthen the salience of the normative goal frame. The study shows how specific intra-organizational cultural beliefs may inhibit the tendency to gossip even in the face of quite severe norm violations in the form of antisocial behavior, that is, bullying at the workplace. Bullying is "an inappropriate but pervasive form of adverse workplace interaction, reflecting sustained efforts by organizational members to harass, attack, or isolate other employees" (De Clercq, 2022). As such, it reflects the kind of deviant behavior that, according to theories of gossip that stress its role as a mechanism of social control, would instigate the victim to retaliate by sanctioning the transgressor, with the spread of negative gossip being one of the potential reactions. This was the core hypothesis of a recent cross-sectional survey study, carried out among 350 Canadian-based employees working full-time in the religious sector (i.e., churches, charities, community organizations, schools) (De Clercq, 2022). The study indeed found statistical evidence for the postulated effect. But it is its other insights that make it particularly relevant for our analysis. A core claim and finding of the study is that there are at least four conditions tempering a victim's propensity to gossip as a result of being bullied: their religiosity, innovation propensity, experienced meaningfulness of work, and trust in top management. From a goal framing perspective, at least two of these four moderators reflect sources strengthening the salience of an employees' normative goal frame in adverse situations.

First, the fact that the study was conducted in religious organizations allows specifying the content of the norms, given the clear expectations, core to most religions, to refrain from all forms of (indirect) aggression: "religiosity could render employees more forgiving of disrespectful treatment from bullies, as well as support their willingness to consider reasons some colleagues might behave in this way" (De Clercq, 2022, p. 4). Hence, compared to less-religious employees, for highly religious ones, the normative expectations related to their faith were salient and more chronically activated.

Second, as discussed in the previous section, trust is inherently based on expectations concerning norms of solidarity and reciprocity, again pointing to a salient normative goal frame buffering the victim's inclination to retaliate with negative gossip as a way to release their frustration.

In sum, a victim's inclination – driven by the hedonic motive to "release their negative energy and feel better about themselves again" (De Clercq, 2022, p. 4) – to spread negative gossip about their bullies is significantly suppressed where context-specific beliefs in the trustworthiness of management and the felt obligation to follow religious norms of non-escalation are salient.

Because the study used self-ratings as measures and did not collect longitudinal data, the correlational findings do not allow us to draw conclusions about causality. In fact, we cannot exclude that being bullied is the result of a victim's previous gossiping. Nevertheless, the study's assumptions and findings nicely illustrate one of our main arguments, according to which an individual's inclination to gossip may be buffered far more often than one would expect based on most theoretical accounts, and that the related mechanisms leading to this restraint follow directly from goal framing mechanisms.

4.1.3 Gossip Cultures

Social contexts, and in particular organizational cultures, can also differ with regard to how prevalent their members believe gossip to be. Settings in which the involved individuals assume that gossip is widespread ("everyone constantly gossips about everyone else") represent strong *gossip cultures*. GFT predicts that the perception that most members will gossip about norm violations pushes the hedonic goal frame into the cognitive background. This will reduce the tendency to shirk because individuals expect to be closely monitored by other members of the organization. This awareness, in turn, will increase the salience of the normative goal frame, because knowledge of and compliance with workplace rules and norms are a precondition for avoiding to be gossiped about. (This makes following norms a matter of expediency rather than a matter of normative obligation.) At the same time, gossip cultures also strengthen the motive to avoid future losses, for example in the form of scorn, disapproval, or withholding of support, thereby increasing the salience of the gain goal frame. Hence, strong gossip cultures strengthen and align the content of the gain and the normative goal frames – "work hard to meet expectations and to avoid potential losses" – implying that it does not matter much which of them is currently in the cognitive foreground.

Investigating the link between gossip prevalence, perceived performance pressure, and psychological well-being, a recent multi-study paper shows that gossip cultures may indeed increase performance, but decrease cooperation sustainability and subjective psychological well-being (Tan et al., 2021). The three different datasets suggest and provide consistent empirical evidence for a complex causal model. It consists of two core predictions. The first one is that employees who believe that the members of their organization frequently share gossip also experience higher levels of performance pressure, which in turn causes them to improve their performance. This effect holds if they assume the gossiping to be mainly negative: perceived positive-gossip prevalence has a much weaker effect on performance pressure. The second prediction states that perceptions of high work-related gossip prevalence decrease employee psychological well-being. The implications of these studies are particularly relevant for our evolutionary goal framing approach to gossip and reputation, because they illustrate how the perception of one's social environment as a "gossip culture" can align all three goal frames.

A first implication, related to perceived negative gossip prevalence decreasing psychological well-being, is that experiencing one's work environment as "gossipy" clearly tempers the hedonic goal frame. This effect sheds light on an important interplay between the hedonic goal frame and the position one occupies in a gossip triad. As we argued earlier in line with Dunbar, participating in the act of sharing gossip as sender or receiver may be triggered by and reinforce the salience of the hedonic goal frame in this particular situation. But as this study suggests, where these situational experiences reflect a pattern that is considered as characteristic for the organization, they are likely to also activate another psychological mechanism, with a more persistent and negative impact on employee well-being. According to the authors, perceived gossip prevalence decreases well-being "due to employees' attentiveness towards the constant monitoring and evaluation by their co-workers, as well as employees' inability to build strong emotional connections, or trusting relationships, with their co-workers" (Tan et al., 2021, p. 423). Knowing that one works in a setting in which everyone constantly gossips about everybody else signals that your colleagues are constantly also watching and talking about you. The negative consequences of being monitored on stress are well documented (Aiello & Kolb, 1995; Davidson & Henderson, 2000). Evidence on other primates also suggests a negative correlation between social monitoring and serotonin levels (Summers et al., 2005; Weinberg-Wolf & Chang, 2019).

A second implication, related to perceived negative-gossip prevalence fostering the experience of work pressure, is that such an organizational gossip culture simultaneously also strengthens the salience of a performance-related normative goal frame and the gain goal frame to preserve or increase one's reputation and work-related resources (or avoid their loss or decline). Knowing that one may easily become the object of gossip raises the awareness that others are constantly evaluating (the quality of) one's work, that they may compare it with the performance of others, and that all this may have repercussions on one's reputation with regard to compliance to professional rules (e.g., competence) and work effort norms (e.g., shirking, performance). A gossip culture and the stress reactions that it elicits instigate safeguarding or improving one's reputation as a good worker and colleague and avoiding the negative evaluations that may damage one's reputation. Since the route to preserving one's reputation (a gain goal) runs through acting according to professional and organizational rules and norms (a normative goal), gossip cultures have the potential to sustain compliance with organizational goals, albeit at the expense of personal psychological well-being.

4.2 Structures

Social structure refers to the patterned social arrangements governing the relations between societal actors. In the course of human evolution, social structures have increased in size and complexity and fluidity. This raises the question to what degree reputation-based gossip mechanisms also hold in the context of these more complex structural arrangements (Soeters & van Iterson, 2002). Whereas for the most part of human history, any interaction took place between natural persons as subjects and objects of an exchange, individuals are increasingly embedded in multiple and nested collectivities. From an evolutionary perspective, with social structures becoming increasingly interdependent and complex, the mechanisms of coalitional computation (Kurzban et al., 2001) will also become increasingly important. Coalitional computation refers to the fact that the cognitive machinery of the human mind evolved to detect coalitional alliances, to "discard ontogenetically long-standing coalitional categorizations in favor of novel ones" (Kurzban et al., 2001), and accordingly switch commitments to new alliances where this yields higher fitness. It implies that humans are sensitive to cues predicting (shifting) individual allegiances.

In the gossip literature, organizations have always been the "natural" testbed for theories of gossip. The organizational environment is, in this respect, unique because it provides a set of clear-cut relationships, roles, and processes that make the gossip process more traceable for scholars who want to test specific hypotheses. Organizations are usually structured around task interdependencies, which come with processes that favor the development of workplace gossip (small scale interactions, intimacy, clear expectations and norms) (Beersma et al., 2019). Formal organizations create special contexts for cooperation, in that they come with a purpose for joint production, have predefined hierarchies, and usually involve some kind of reward in exchange for effort of its members. Gossip studies investigated the influence of dependence (especially in power and status hierarchies) and interdependence (task, friendship, and trust) relationships. Current research features influential social-structural explanations of gossip and cooperation that were originally developed for and investigated mainly in small close-knit (rural) communities (Scott, 2008b). The question is whether the gossip mechanisms of mutual monitoring and social control as they were found to sustain cooperation in small-scale communities also do so in such formal organizational settings.

4.2.1 Dependence Structures

Dependence can take many forms. An important one is power based on functional dependence. Its most visible examples are formal hierarchies in which higher-level positions have the formal right to take and implement decisions that have consequences for those lower in the hierarchy. But power relations based on functional dependence can also emerge among equals. For example, individuals may acquire higher status and prestige because they have skills or resources that are highly valued in a setting and in scarce supply. Where professional expertise is scarce, advice from the more knowledgeable becomes precious and tends to be reciprocated by deference and respect (Agneessens & Wittek, 2012; Blau, 1963). Both situations create power imbalances, with power being defined as the inverse of dependence (Emerson, 1962). Dependence can also have cognitive-affective sources, such as reliance on socio-emotional support.

An influential argument draws a straightforward connection between joint dependence and gossiping. According to this *weapon of the weak* thesis

(Scott, 2008a, 2018b), being jointly dependent on a powerful actor creates a mutual interest to share information, and gossip and slander allow the building and strengthening of protective coalitions among the weaker parties. Gossip among equals in subordinate or marginal positions can be an effective "everyday form of resistance" to destroy the reputation of more powerful individuals because the gossipers, operating under the radar, cannot be held accountable (Brison, 1992; Scott, 2008b; Wickham, 1998).

An implicit assumption in this argument is that occupying the same (subordinate) position in the social structure is sufficient to create the mutual trust that is necessary to engage in the potentially risky endeavor of exposing one's critical stance toward the powerful. Whereas this assumption may be justified for the settings for which this hypothesis was developed – that is, small-scale (rural) communities and their historically ingrained and stable patron–client authority structures – GFT suggests that this may not hold in more complex contemporary settings, because two conditions are likely to undermine the basis for oppositional solidarity. First, functional and hierarchical differentiation is higher, resulting in a multitude of positions and differential allegiances with those in power. Second, group memberships tend to be less stable.

Functional dependence on the potential object of gossip, or interdependence with potential gossip receivers and objects, strengthens the salience of the gain goal frame (or the related focus on avoiding losses). Strong dependence comes with the powerful party having many opportunities to cause severe damage to the weaker parties. Awareness of such vulnerabilities and the externalities that they may cause will shift the focus to the avoidance of potential futures losses, and also fosters forward-looking, calculated moves geared to preserve one's own resources (Giardini & Wittek, 2019b). The deterring effect of such dependence relations, therefore, is likely to inhibit taking risky moves, including spreading negative evaluations about the powerful – unless solidarity and trust relations with one's peers happen to be strong enough to push the gain goal frame into the background, thereby reducing the perceived risk of sharing sensitive evaluations about the powerful. In sum, a goal framing perspective suggests that strong joint dependencies on the powerful are likely to decrease the likelihood of negative gossip where the level of trust in others (in particular peers) is low and increase it where trust is high.

How such goal framing processes can affect gossip behavior in such dependence relations is illustrated by two studies, situated at different levels of analysis. Both show that the stronger the joint dependence on powerful actors, and the lower the trust in others, the less likely the powerful will become the object of gossip. The first study contrasts (changes in) the personal networks of citizens of the former German Democratic Republic (GDR) (East Germany) with those of the Federal Republic of Germany (West Germany) (Völker & Flap, 2001). An important characteristic of the GDR's "formal" structure was the power of its Ministry for State Security, which in its heydays employed more than 90,000 "regular" civil servants and, during its whole period of existence more than 620,000 "unofficial" collaborators (also called "secret informers" until 1968). The latter were not formally "employed" by the ministry, operated undercover, and reported about the behavior of citizens in their direct personal environments, such as neighbors, friends, colleagues, but also family members. The major purpose of this web of informants was to identify citizens with "subversive" attitudes and intentions. Being under suspicion could have severe consequences for the respective citizens and their families, such as losing career opportunities

The web of unofficial collaborators covered all societal domains and had become the major pillar of the rule by the Socialist Party. The power of the Ministry for State Security, as well as the widespread presence of undercover informants was well known in the general population of the GDR, and it had a major impact on the patterns of personal relations and gossip behavior. With an average of eleven contacts, personal networks of East Germans in 1989 were surprisingly small – similar studies in the Netherlands and the United States revealed personal networks of almost double this size. Two segregated social circles constituted the social-capital base of citizens of the former GDR: the members of the "niche," and those forming the provision network. The networks were segregated in the sense that what was exchanged in one network would not be exchanged in the other. The niche was built on a small number of contacts (2.6 on average, with a standard deviation of 1.6) with whom one discussed political matters. The relations were characterized by very strong interpersonal trust. Niches were very dense, "remarkably close, multiplex, characterized by repeated transactions and with high educational and occupational similarity" (Völker & Flap, 2001, p. 423). In contrast, the provision network was built around weak, uniplex ties to people who could help with the provision of scarce items. These network patterns reflect citizens' efforts to "avoid the adverse effects of institutional conditions" (Völker & Flap, 2001, p. 423). Sensitive information about third parties (bosses, politicians) was shared only in the niche.

The relative impact that the formal power structure of a political regime and the related cultural beliefs exerted on citizens' communication behavior becomes even more visible when analyzing the networks after the fall of the wall in 1994. More than a third of niche relations became weaker, and most of them decreased in multiplicity. Moreover, whereas niche relations were still strongly based on talking about politics, this was no longer systematically linked to also sharing personal matters – which before the revolution was crucial to establish the mutual trust that it takes to engage in risky discussions.

This comparison of the institutional effects on social relations and the related patterns of communication, including sharing sensitive third-party information, again shows that gossiping as a potential tool of social control might be a far less widespread and effective "weapon of the weak" than previous theorizing suggests. In the case of the former GDR at least, gossip exchanges about sensitive political or professional contacts likely were restricted to an average of three to five trusted and very close contacts who often also tended to be part of a densely knit clique. Whatever inclination they might have felt to vent their grievances about wrongdoings of specific others, the salient concern to preserve their resources and avoid sanctions for the members of their social circle might have kept citizens of the GDR from openly and widely damaging the reputations of others.

The second study also illustrates that sharing gossip about the powerful is also not an automatism in organizations, as becomes evident in a sociometric survey carried out among the employees of a medium-sized Dutch nonprofit child care organization. It assessed to what degree two types of trust affected the inclination to talk about the boss: *generalized* trust in management and in one's colleagues, and *interpersonal trust* relationships with one's direct supervisor and with one's colleagues. One part of the study collected information about the informal social relations among employees at two sites ("Blue" and "Orange") of the organization. The sites were identical in terms of hierarchical structure tasks and number of employees. Both settings' informal structure showed notable similarities in several respects: each employee had an average number of ten friendly relations and mentioned about 2.5 gossip partners. At the group level, both sites exhibit similar densities of friendship and gossip networks and similar average ratings for the quality of the relation with the site manager, and all but one of the twenty-nine respondents at each site indicated that they are involved in gossip. Given these similarities, the three main differences in the informal social structures of the two sites are even more striking.

First, at the Blue Site, more than half of all gossip content was negative, compared to 12 percent at the Orange Site. Moreover, whereas only a little more than 1 percent of gossip was positive at the Blue Site; this figure climbed to 28 percent at the Orange Site. Second, there was a stunning difference in the frequency and structure of communication ties. Whereas the average number of frequently (three times or more) contacted colleagues per employee at the Blue Site was about 10, this number was 23 at the Orange Site. The respective densities of the communication networks were 0.33 at the Blue Site and 0.72 at the Orange Site. Third, there was a significant difference in the average frequency of contacts with the site manager, with the manager at the Blue Site, where negative gossip prevailed, having more communication ties than the manager at the Orange Site.

The findings point to the importance of disentangling different dimensions of the informal structure, given that the social mechanisms triggered by interpersonal trust and communication relations are not the same. A particularly noteworthy finding is that the incidence of negative gossip about the boss was lower in the group where communication frequency and density was extraordinarily high. The study hypothesized and found that negative gossip about the boss becomes much more likely if generalized trust in management is low and if trust in colleagues is high, with both conditions also mutually reinforcing each other. However, despite the effect of low generalized trust in management on negative gossip about the boss being smaller, high trust in colleagues was not a necessary precondition.

With the effect size of low generalized trust in management being more than twice as large as generalized trust in colleagues, it can be concluded that distrust in management is the main trigger for negative gossip about the boss. This effect is further enhanced when contacts between employees are trusting and frequent. But whereas low generalized trust in management turned out to be the strongest predictor of negative gossip about the boss, the analysis also revealed that low generalized trust in management did not systematically increase the likelihood of gossiping about *one's own supervisor*.

4.2.2 Coalition Structures

GFT predicts that coalition structures increase the likelihood of third-party gossip. A coalition structure reflects a relational pattern in which two persons are linked through a strong bond, and have a bad relationship with the same third party or parties. Such triadic configurations represent the structural equivalent of a strong ingroup–outgroup distinction. A strong bond will favor the tendency to gossip about third parties disliked by both. In such cases, the absence of a strong personal tie with the third party reduces the normative obligations that would temper the inclination to damage their reputations. Gain and hedonic concerns may take over when sharing negative information about this person. Another consequence of the joint occurrence of strong ingroup solidarity ties and strong negative outgroup relations is that they align the three overarching goal frames to the detriment of cooperation with the outgroup: gossiping about outgroup members not only strengthens the hedonic goal frame, it also reinforces ingroup solidarity norms, and the related vigilance to potential third-party threats to the ingroup may preserve or even increase the resource base of the ingroup, thereby also activating the gain frame.

A social network study carried out among 220 employees of 6 organizations and among 104 students of 6 classes of a Dutch business school revealed striking similarities in the triadic social structures favoring the tendency to gossip (Wittek & Wielers, 1998). The analyses revealed that in all twelve units (departments and classes), coalition structures were the main predictor for the tendency to gossip. The detection of this coalition effect is particularly important because two other triadic structures that could provide plausible alternative explanations did not show significant associations with the tendency to gossip. One of them is triadic closure, that is, all three individuals in the triad being connected through a strong interpersonal relationship. The other one is the classical brokerage relationship, with the broker having close ties to two other individuals who are not connected. Neither cohesive nor brokerage structures had a significant effect on the inclination to gossip.

The strong effect of coalition structures also aligns with insights on the evolutionary importance of coalitional computation for human cooperation as it was introduced above (Kurzban et al., 2001).

4.2.3 Cohesive Structures

GFT's predictions are at odds with one of the core claims linking social structure to gossip and cooperation; that is, that negative gossip flourishes in strong personal relations and close-knit networks (Borgatti & Foster, 2003). This argument suggests that the strength of personal relations is usually grounded in cognitive-affective interdependence – such as friendship or strong interpersonal trust relations. Given the potential risks associated with leaking gossip, the high level of trust and solidarity that comes with this kind of interdependence ensures discretion. Furthermore, gossip becomes an effective instrument of social control in particular in small-scale communities whose members are closely knit together through such webs of interdependence, because such structures allow for mutual monitoring (Coleman, 1990; Elias & Scotson, 1994; Ellickson, 2009).

GFT argues that, if hedonic motives are indeed the default trigger for gossiping, then it is likely that individuals are also willing to engage in gossiping with individuals with whom they might not (yet) have a close interpersonal trust relationship (and of course they may calibrate the content and severity of the evaluations accordingly). Second, since close interpersonal trust relations also come with solidarity norms (prescribing to avoid damaging the other) and remedial norms (prescribing not to talk behind the back of a close relation), it is unlikely that friends will badmouth a third party whom both would consider a close friend (Giardini & Wittek, 2019b). Hence, close-knit social structures strengthen the normative goal frame, pushing the hedonic goal frame into the background and thereby tempering the inclination to gossip about each other.

Much available evidence indeed shows a substantial correlation between the strength of a relation and the exchange of gossip, thereby lending some support to the original proposition that closeness breeds gossip. But this does not imply that people gossip only with friends. Friendship or strong interpersonal trust is not a precondition for gossiping. This is the conclusion of a longitudinal network study on the role that gossip plays in the emergence of friendship and interpersonal trust and vice versa (Ellwardt et al., 2012). Employees of three departments of a Dutch childcare organization were followed over a period of one and a half years. During three measurement waves, employees provided detailed sociometric information about their interpersonal trust relations in the department, but also with whom they gossiped. Whereas having a friendship relation indeed increased the likelihood of gossiping, gossip between two unrelated individuals increased the likelihood of a friendship forming between them. However, individuals with disproportionately high gossip activity had fewer friends in the network, suggesting that the use of gossiping to attract friends has a limit. Hence, closeness indeed is not a necessary condition for gossiping, as predicted by GFT.

Sharing potentially sensitive third-party information not only may come with the warm glow involved in personal bonding, but it also has a strong relational signaling effect: it makes the gossip sender vulnerable *because* the receiver may leak the information, and it also reveals information about the senders' position in their social network. At the same time, sharing gossip functions as the sender's sounding device: should the gossip become known to others, this demonstrates that the receiver is not trustworthy. This signaling mechanism rests on two assumptions. The first one is that the sender is likely to calibrate the sensitivity of the shared information depending on the phase of the relationship, starting with relatively harmless information. Second, the relative potential damage of sharing low-level gossip with an acquaintance is much lower than the potential damage that can be inflicted upon us by somebody with whom we have a long-standing strong relationship (and who therefore has far more knowledge about us and our deeds).

The fine-grained relational information of this study shows that receiving gossip from specific others can be interpreted as a signal of trust and the intention to build and intensify a personal relationship. In this case, it increases the salience of the normative goal frame of the receiver, thereby fostering cognitive-affective interdependence.

4.3 Dispositions

Although GFT predicts that the three goal frames differ in their a priori strength, with the normative goal frame having the lowest a priori salience and the hedonic goal frame the highest, the related saliences differ across individuals.

People differ in terms of individual-level dispositions, that is, constellations of relatively stable personality traits that influence a person's behavior such that it remains consistent across different situations. Such interindividual variations in dispositions can have evolutionary advantages (Wilson, 1998).

Depending on the kind of individual disposition, it may make somebody, on average, more or less prone to pursue hedonic, gain, or normative goals. That is, an individual disposition may raise or lower the relative a priori salience of a specific goal frame. As a result, contextual or situational cues may be less influential in affecting the salience of an individual's goal frames.

4.3.1 Social Value Orientations

Individuals can be distinguished based on their social value orientation (Murphy et al., 2011; Van Lange, 1999), meaning that there are four different categories of people: altruists, prosocials, individualists, and competitors. This typology reflects the idea that individuals may fundamentally differ with regard to whose payoffs they tend to maximize in dealings with others, independently of the setting in which they find themselves. Competitors go for getting the most out of a situation for themselves and at the same time reducing the potential benefits that their exchange partners may acquire. Individualists try to increase their own benefits, but don't care about payoffs of the partner. Prosocials are motivated by increasing the benefits for themselves *and* for others. Finally, altruists are keen to improve the situation of others at their, the altruists', expense. Hence, whereas the same situational cue may immediately trigger a frame switch from, say, a salient gain to a salient normative goal frame in individuals with a prosocial disposition, this may not be the case or take much longer for individuals with a competitive disposition.

The effect of social value orientation on the a priori salience of goal frames is nicely illustrated by an experimental study on the interplay between a proself vs. prosocial orientation, an individual's power, and gossip (Jeuken et al., 2015). Two findings are particularly relevant in the context of our argument. First, if in a position of power, prosocials are less likely to gossip, whereas proselfs are more likely to do so (Jeuken et al., 2015). The prosocial disposition tempers both the hedonic and the gain goal frame that usually is a correlate of occupying power positions, whereas the proself disposition exacerbates them. If in a position of low power, an individual's tendency to gossip depends on the other party's social value orientation: low-power individuals were more likely to engage in gossiping vis-a-vis high-power counterparts with a competitive orientation than vis-a-vis high-power counterparts with a prosocial orientation. This finding is particularly instructive for understanding goal framing processes. It suggests that behavioral cues signaling the salience of either a gain or a normative goal frame have a strong impact on the salience of the respective goal frames of interaction partners. The influence of other people's behavior may even outweigh the effect of their stronger structural position.

4.3.2 Primary and Secondary Psychopathy

Another class of individual dispositions is captured by the so-called Dark Triad. It consists of what scholars call primary and secondary psychopathy, *narcissism* and *Machiavellianism*. A study investigated how scoring high on these traits influences the motivations to gossip (Lyons & Hughes, 2015). Dark Triad dispositions have been argued to be evolutionarily adaptive cheater strategies in contexts where the related manipulative strategies are difficult to detect. The study consisted of an online survey among 372 participants, of which 76 were men. Four different gossip motives were distinguished: information gathering, social enjoyment, negative influence, and group protection. Each of these dimensions was measured with a set of statements. For each of these statements, respondents were asked to what degree they agreed having engaged in the respective behavior in the past. For example: "For me a reason to instigate this conversation was [to damage the reputation of the person we talked about], or [to protect the person I was talking with against the person we were talking about]." This measurement allows one to disentangle gossip that is mainly driven by hedonic motives ("social enjoyment") from gossip rooted in gain or normative motives ("negative influence," "group protection"). The findings showed that *all* Dark Triad dispositions have a significant and positive effect on negative influence gossip, and no systematic association with information gathering gossip. Social enjoyment and group protection gossip was practiced by individuals scoring high on narcissism and (primary) psychopathy – but not by Machiavellians. Another important finding is the positive association between secondary psychopathy and group protection gossip. According to the authors, this reflects earlier findings according to which individuals with this trait "have other-oriented emotions intact, especially with regards to people who are considered as ingroup members" (Lyons & Hughes, 2015, p. 2), and "can be induced to feel concern towards ingroup members" (p. 2). This makes social-protection gossip an effective tool for Machiavellians to elicit cooperation from others. Another online survey (Hartung et al., 2019), which was interested in whether the link between dark triad dispositions and the six gossip motives differed between private and work settings, further refines these insights. In work settings, Machiavellianism was the only Dark Triad disposition systematically associated with negative influence gossip, whereas it was the sole predictor of information gathering and protection gossip.

Taken together, these patterns suggest that there is at least one distinct personality type, Machiavellians, whose gossiping interventions are driven almost exclusively by a salient gain goal frame, and for whom neither normative nor hedonic motives play an important role when discussing evaluative information about third parties. They may also be the ones whose gossiping behaviors may be least subject to variations in the institutional environments or situations, whereas this is likely to be the case for individuals scoring high on secondary psychopathology traits. For a discussion positioning Machiavellianism in evolutionary biology and personality psychology, see Wilson et al. (1996).

In sum, variations in individual dispositions are likely to result in inter-individual differences in the a priori salience of the three overarching goal frames and will therefore also impact gossip behavior. According to GFT, frame switches from gain to normative may "happen" even to individuals with a strongly competitive disposition, as the reverse may be the case for individuals with a strong prosocial disposition. Individuals can differ in terms of how inclined they are, on average, toward hedonic, gain, or normative behavior. But GFT also suggests that these orientations are not immutable and may eventually switch. When such switches will occur depends on the kind and constellation of cues that individuals experience in a given situation.

4.4 Situations

For human-motivated cognition, there is an important distinction to be made between contextual and situational factors. Though both are interrelated, are often used interchangeably, and jointly define the "situatedness" (Rehm et al., 2003) of behavior, they are not the same. Disentangling variations in situatedness and the interplay between context and situation is key to GFT. Situations can provide very strong cues triggering frame switches and changes in behavior. These cues *may* override individual dispositions, but also beliefs or preferences rooted in the respective institutional or cultural contexts. Despite the well-documented power of situational cues to overrule even strong contextual (institutional) constraints, surprisingly little effort has been made to disentangle the two, both theoretically and empirically. This certainly holds for research on gossip, where lumping contextual and situational conditions may lead to misinterpretations. Given GFT's strong emphasis on the impact of situational variations, it is worthwhile to explore some examples that allow us to disentangle the related dynamics in some more detail. Two aspects of situations are particularly relevant as antecedents to gossip because of their effect on the salience of particular goal frames: the perceived severity of a norm violation and its signaling character.

4.4.1 Severity of Norm Violations

The notion of *situational strength* captures the range of behaviors that are considered as appropriate in a given situation (Gelfand & Lun, 2013). Situations that are perceived as strong come with a restricted range of acceptable behaviors, and they leave less room for individual discretion with regard to how to react to violations of these expectations. This means that strong situations strengthen the salience of the normative goal frame. Hence, they reinforce both the shared cultural expectations about what kind of behavior is appropriate or not appropriate, and how one should respond to such behavior. Evidence shows that when evaluating (norm violating) behavior of others, situational strength matters more for collectivist cultures than for individualist cultures (Choi & Nisbett, 1998; Morris & Peng, 1994). Collectivist beliefs strengthen the a priori salience of the normative goal frame prescribing *strong direct sanctions* against norm violators (second-order cooperation). This mechanism may explain the unexpected *negative* correlation between collectivistic cultural beliefs and perceived gossip appropriateness as an informal sanction, as it was detected by Eriksson et al. (2021). Their research was based on a cross-national scenario study among a convenience sample of 22,863 students in 57 countries (Eriksson et al., 2021). Respondents were presented with ten different situations describing different types of norm violations, from neglecting a norm requiring contributions to a common resource, to violations of "meta-norms," such as physical aggression as an overreaction to a verbal insult. Respondents rated the degree of (in)appropriateness of each norm violation, as well as the appropriateness of four types of reactions to such norm violations: verbal confrontations, gossip, social ostracism (avoiding the norm violator in the future), and nonaction. Statistical analyses show that the more severe someone perceives a norm violation, the less doing nothing is considered as legitimate and the more direct verbal confrontation is valued as a reaction. This was followed by gossip and social ostracism. Eriksson et al. (2021) see this pattern as an indicator of a cultural universal: the more severe a norm violation is perceived to be, the more likely it is that one or more of these three reactions are used to informally sanction the transgressor. This holds both for violations of cooperation norms as for uncivil behavior.

According to Eriksson et al. (2021), one of the most intriguing unexpected findings of their study is that appropriateness ratings of gossip were higher in countries with strong individualist belief systems (and lower in countries with collectivist belief systems). This finding poses a puzzle given earlier claims that gossip is less likely in individualist than in collectivist cultures. In their discussion of the unexpected finding, Eriksson and colleagues ponder that it may be related to which kinds of behavior a culture considers to be a "punishment." An important difference between gossip and other strategies is that the former involves interaction with other persons than the norm violator, whereas confrontation (physical and verbal sanctions) does not. In contrast, active avoidance (social ostracism) involves behavior related to how one interacts with the norm violator. Such direct sanctions might therefore be perceived as stronger and more effective, and in turn may be considered as more appropriate reactions for severe norm violations. If this assumption holds and collectivist or tight cultures also tend to be less forgiving toward norm violations than members of individualist or loose cultures, then it follows that in these cultures we find a positive association with direct sanctions and a negative correlation with gossip. The significant negative correlation between "cultural tightness" and gossip that the study also found is in line with this interpretation.

4.4.2 Signaling Value of Norm Violations

Norm violations may not only differ in terms of their perceived severity. They may also vary with regard to their meaning, or what they signal about the (changing) salience of the normative goal frame of the transgressor. According to GFT, how individuals react to norm violations depends on whether the norm violators' behavior, in the eyes of others, signals a declining general motivation to comply with the solidarity norms holding for the (work) group, or whether they should be seen as a mishap, that is, that the breach was not intentional (Lindenberg, 2002). An important implication of this claim is that individuals may show strong negative reactions to relatively minor norm violations, and they may show relatively mild reactions to major infractions. This proposition was tested in a study among nineteen members of a management team of a paper factory (Wittek, 2013). Each member was presented with eight vignettes, each describing a different norm violation by a colleague. Descriptions systematically varied with regard to the *frequency* (whether the norm violation happened only once, that is, it was unique, or had already recurred several times), and *scope* (whether it affected only one colleague or the whole group). The *severity* of the norm violation was assessed by letting respondents rank the eight situations in this dimension. Participants could rate for each situation how appropriate they considered each of twelve different types of (direct and indirect) informal reactions. An important finding was that gossiping, together with retaliation, ostracism, and doing nothing did not differ much in terms of the negative appropriateness scores they received. In contrast, direct reactions were considered as appropriate. But what triggers the use of sanctions that are generally considered as inappropriate? According to GFT, behaviors that signal somebody's low concern for the norms in place also diminish the salience of the observers' normative goal frame (Keizer et al., 2008). If this reasoning holds, then the same type of norm violation should elicit different kinds of reactions, depending on the alleged strength of the normative mindset of the violator. This is exactly what the study found, using the frequency of the violation of the same norm by the same person as an indicator that may signal the violator's waning normative commitment. Statistical analyses (carried out on 152 "sanctioning decisions" nested in eight situations and 19 managers) showed that the frequency of norm violations was the *only* predictor that had a significant and very strong positive effect on indirect sanctions and hence gossiping. The finding is particularly noteworthy because neither the perceived severity of the norm violation nor its scope (i.e., whether it had negative repercussions only on one team member or affected the whole team or factory) was systematically related to indirect reactions to norm violations. This implies that what triggers gossiping in this team was what the norm violation signaled in terms of the salience of the normative mindset of who committed it. It is not the severity of the infraction or its consequences.

The revealed pattern also has another implication. In the literature analyzing the role of punishment in sustaining cooperation, gossip is generally perceived as a low-threshold activity, cheap to administer and effective in its potential outcomes (Ellickson, 2009; Guala, 2012). The findings reported here put this interpretation into perspective, at least for the team under study. The common reaction to norm violations is that the grievance is brought up openly, either bilaterally or in a group meeting. In contrast, gossip and third-party involvement appear such as a move of last resort, which will be used only if one has reason to doubt the norm violators' sustained commitment to comply with the group's professional and informal normative expectations. Finally, this study also illustrates that it is not only the goal frames of a potential gossip sender that matter, but also how these potential gossip mongers assess the salience of the goal frames of potential gossip targets.

4.5 Conclusions

This section applied a goal framing perspective to explain under which conditions gossip has reputation effects on cooperation in modern societies. We argued that for this to happen, gossip needs to be driven by a normative mindset. We then elaborated on four sets of conditions that may affect goal frame salience: cultural beliefs, formal and informal structural arrangements, individual dispositions, and situational differences. In many cases, our goal framing predictions suggest that previous theorizing needs to be refined; in other cases, our goal framing predictions contradict established propositions.

With regard to culture, our goal framing approach casts doubts on the *collectivism breeds gossip* argument. Instead, we show that existing evidence on contemporary societies is much more in line with GFT's prediction of a negative correlation between collectivism and gossiping, with a strong moderating role of situational differences: collectivist cultures favor direct rather than indirect reactions to norm violations.

For structural explanations, GFT and the related evidence offer a more refined view on the influential *weapon of the weak* and the *cohesion breeds gossip* arguments. Gossip, of course, may be used as a weapon of the weak, but occupying a subordinate position is not sufficient to instigate negative gossip about higher-ups. Interpersonal trust is an important condition for this to happen. In organizational settings, employees gossip about management in particular if generalized trust in management is low. But employees are still very reluctant to gossip about their own supervisor. Strong interpersonal trust also breeds gossip about peers – but usually about third parties who are distrusted by both the gossip sender and receiver. As predicted by GFT, coalitions, not cohesion, breed gossip and the related reputation effects on cooperation.

Individual dispositions too affect goal frame salience and therefore gossip behavior. Prosocial value orientations temper the gain orientation that usually comes with power positions, and therefore also reduce the inclination to gossip. Proself orientations do the opposite. Psychopathologies, such as Machiavellianism, boost the gain goal frame and trigger negative gossip. No empirical studies were found that assess the interplay of individual dispositions and gossip with reputations and cooperation.

Finally, situational differences matter. This holds in particular for the perceived severity and signaling value of norm violations. The link between perceived severity of norm violations and the perceived appropriateness of direct (rather than indirect) forms of punishment seems to hold across cultural contexts. Nevertheless, the presumed motive behind the norm violation seems to be a more important predictor for gossiping than its severity. Individuals are more inclined to gossip if the norm violation is perceived as signaling a transgressor's weak or declining normative mindset.

To conclude, this section developed novel hypotheses about the goal framing processes through which four classes of antecedents affect gossip and its potential reputation effects on cooperation. The technological progress of the past half century, exemplified by breakthroughs in information and communication technology (ICT) and the World Wide Web, has given rise to yet another class of antecedents with major implications for gossip, reputation, and cooperation. This is what we turn to in the next section.

5 Gossip and Reputation in Contemporary Societies

Gossip "is a means of social control, a sanction that forces one to adhere more closely to social norms than one would otherwise be inclined. Reputation is determined by gossip, and the casual conversations of others affect one's relative standing and one's acceptability as a mate or as a partner in social exchange" (Barkow, 1992, p. 628). What happens when the casual conversations characterized by privacy and some form of intimacy are transformed into a digital metric designed to reward or punish strangers' behaviors in online environments? What happens to gossip when targets use social media to publicly share behaviors and choices that in the past were supposed to be private and accessible only to a few people through gossip? Has the Internet changed the cultures, structures, and relationships in such a way that gossip and reputation have become something completely different?

In the last twenty-five years the opportunities offered by the digital world (online reputations, recommendation systems, social media, peer-to-peer systems, etc.) to share information boundlessly, to allow anyone to create and share content, to overcome physical boundaries in economic transactions and product availability, have led to an unprecedented interest in the workings of reputation. These technological innovations have had a significant impact on our opportunities to connect, communicate, coordinate, and cooperate. Most notable among these innovations are, first, the implementation of the World Wide Web and the related tools, which range from portable computers and smartphones to the Internet of Things. Second, the social technologies that these infrastructures enable, in particular what now is commonly referred to as "social media": communication platforms that allow billions of individuals and organizations to share information, and allow people to build online worlds that can potentially be accessed by anybody, anytime. Third, there is the related software shaping our informational environment, such as algorithms selecting who receives which news and when, resulting, for example, in differential exposure to specific information for large parts of the population (the so-called "echo chambers," Flaxman et al., 2016).

A common thread running through academic and nonacademic work on reputation in the digital age is that the Internet has offered exceptional opportunities for the circulation of information, while posing equally unprecedented threats. The amount of information available is extraordinary, but this can make access to reliable and useful knowledge much more difficult, at the same time raising concerns about privacy, data use, and long-term consequences. Masum and Tovey (2011) claim that reputation systems, if properly designed,

> have the potential to reshape society for the better by shining the light of accountability into dark places, through the mediated judgments of billions of people worldwide, to create what we call the Reputation Society (Masum & Zhang, 2004). A key concern of the Reputation Society is the need to deal with information overload. When anything can be broadcast and accessed, filtering becomes essential (Shenk, 1997). Worse yet, long-term civic issues can become lost in a constant stream of short-term distractions. How do we find what is relevant and worth acting on? (Masum & Tovey, 2011, xvi)

According to one estimate, "more than a billion people now spend at least an hour a day on social media" (Crockett, 2017, p. 1), and the amount of content produced and shared is huge. Gossip research has not kept pace with these developments, resulting in a relative paucity of theories and evidence about the potential implications of this new environment (with a few exceptions on gossip in virtual worlds, Gabriels & De Backer, 2016, and online celebrity gossip, Meyers, 2010).

In this section we will discuss the digital world as a new kind of evolutionary environment in which the usual conditions supporting a normative goal frame in gossiping, thoroughly analyzed in the previous section, are replaced by a different set of elements. Formulated in goal framing terms, some features of digital environments may reinforce the hedonic goal frame and also take away some of the normative constraints that govern gossip in face-to-face offline interactions. The question we intend to answer is: Can gossip support cooperation through reputation effects in a world in which information production, sharing, and its consequences have profoundly changed?

5.1 Technology as an Extension of the Physical World

We posit that the digital world creates a new environment characterized by new opportunities for social interactions. The resulting changes in situations, structures, and cultures may affect the salience of goal frames differently, while at the same time transforming the meaning of gossip and, mostly, reputation. In this new reality, technology makes visible and publicly available information about events, behaviors, and attitudes that in the offline world are shared only in a closed and private environment.

Here, we identify three different ways in which digital environments were hypothesized to influence gossip, reputation, and cooperation. The first line of investigation assumes that offline patterns of gossiping and the conditions that affect it will replicate in online environments. This perspective sees digital environments as a mere extension of offline environments. The technological means enrich the repertoire of communication, for example, by adding speed and the possibility to interact with a large number of people at the same time, but the mechanisms driving gossip behavior and its consequences essentially remain the same. For example, investigating social media use of adolescents in the United States, Danah Boyd writes: "Social media mirror, magnify and extend everyday social worlds . . . By and large, teens use social media to do what they have been doing" (Boyd, 2008, p. 27). For gossip, this means that online activities themselves – such as who posts what, about whom, and how on a social media site such as Facebook – become issues for moralization and norm affirmation, just such as any other third-party behavior. The difference is that communication takes place through instant messaging on another platform (Jones et al., 2011). A similar argument suggesting that online communication is the extension of real-world gossip behavior has also been proposed for organizational settings. Analyzing 520,000 emails sent by 151 individuals between 1997 and 2002 and involving Enron employees, Mitra and Gilbert (2012) identified 7,200 messages that they classified as gossip emails. These are messages that contain the name of a person who is not in the list of recipients. Many of their findings reflect patterns that had already been identified in earlier studies: employees gossip mostly with others of the same rank; the majority of employees dedicate a small proportion of emails to gossip; and the valence is predominantly neutral.

A second perspective suggests that digital environments will amplify certain cognitive-emotional reactions, thereby undermining cooperation sustainability. For instance, Kock (2004) argued that stimuli coming with human face-to-face communication would play an essential role in inducing the inclination toward gossiping, thereby facilitating predictions about how other people will behave in specific situations. Instead, the suppression of face-to-face communication might reduce the inclination to gossip. In an ethnographic study of the use of gossip in a virtual world (i.e., the platform Second Life), Gabriels and De Backer (2016) show that there are many overlaps between online and offline gossip concerning uses and functions. At the same time, technology offers new possibilities to exploit gossip, such as logging the evidence in order to spot cheaters, thus making online gossip an "inflated form of traditional gossip."

The third perspective predicts that digital environments providing reputational information are detrimental for cooperation, but argues that this is due to the fact that they provide access to highly accurate information about the social network of other individuals. Studies of online gossip networks reflect the offline differences between collectivist and individualist personal network structures (Na et al., 2015), pointing to the importance of cultural beliefs in shaping network patterns also online. That is, the dense Facebook network of someone who was born and lives in a collectivist Asian country should become less dense and more centralized in case this person moves to and lives for a longer period in, say, the United States. Interestingly enough, with regard to Asians moving to the United States, the statistical tests did not find evidence for this hypothesis. Na, Kosinski, and Stillwell (2015) speculate that this might be due to the fact that these individuals may easily find and select into one of the many Asian communities in the United States, which allows them to maintain their cultural traditions. In contrast, some weak statistical correlation was found for the personal Facebook networks of Americans who moved to Asian countries becoming less centralized. These findings suggest that the relational patterns of persons with individualist cultural origins are less likely to persist once they find themselves living in collectivist cultures, whereas the opposite does not hold.

Whether technology is an extension of the physical world or we live in a new socio-technical reality, the question remains of how gossip supports cooperation thanks to the activation of a normative goal frame.

5.1.1 The Increased Salience of the Hedonic Goal Frame in the Online World

Even if online interactions lack some of the defining features of gossip, for example, intimacy, and an absent third party, it is still important to understand which goal frames are made salient and what consequences this might have on cooperation. Online environments exacerbate reactions to moral outrage. They are likely to distort gossip's "traditional" use as a tool to promote cooperation in small-scale settings through the spread of reputational information about norm violators. The Internet has significantly altered not only our exposure to norm violations and how we perceive and react to them, but also the personal and societal costs and benefits of our responses (Crockett, 2017).

The Internet increases our exposure to moral wrongdoings and other people's emotional reactions to them. Digital platforms such as the microblogging site Twitter have made the expression of moral outrage costless, universal, and with way fewer repercussions than the offline world (Crockett, 2017). Online platforms promote content that is likely to be shared, and since this holds for information eliciting moral outrage, we are more likely to be exposed to immoral acts in online environments than in the offline world. This is one of the findings of an event-sampling study in which a diverse sample of 1,252

North American adults was asked to report their moral experiences, five times a day during a three-day period (Crockett, 2017). Whereas almost 30 percent of the participants indicated that they had learned about an immoral act online, less than 25 percent reported that they came to know this in a personal encounter, and only 10 percent said that they acquired such information through traditional media. As for reactions to online exposure to moral wrongdoings: the study also found significant differences in the intensity of self-reported anger and disgust as a reaction to immoral acts encountered in online environments. The study speculates about some other possible implications. Since digital media also makes it easier to express one's anger, digital media may also result in a self-reinforcing cycle of "anger begetting more anger." In line with this reinforcement argument, another study, analyzing 12.7 million tweets of 7,331 users, showed that positive social feedback for expressing one's outrage increases the likelihood that someone shows moral outrage in the future (Brady et al., 2021).

This hedonic frame could also be supported by the gain goal frame, if we consider moral outrage as a form of virtue signaling that will benefit one's reputation (Crockett, 2017). Compared to offline reactions such as gossip, shaming, or punishment, the expression of online moral outrage increases the potential benefits as they come with public virtue signaling, while at the same time reducing the risk for retaliation and decreasing empathic distress that usually accompanies the act of actively punishing somebody. Exposure to online environments has the potential to strengthen the salience of the hedonic goal frame, given the almost costless opportunities to engage and the built-in positive reinforcement cycles this produces. Furthermore, increased exposure to moral wrongdoings and other people's emotional reactions to them also aligns both: the normative background goal that legitimizes punishing norm violators and the gain that comes with the reputational rewards that can be gained from publicly broadcasting one's virtuousness.

5.1.2 The Gain Goal Frame in Social Network Platforms

Accurate knowledge of a group's network structure may undermine cooperation sustainability because the availability of this information may create incentives for opportunistic behavior (Larson, 2016), thereby pushing the gain goal frame of group members into the cognitive foreground. Social networking platforms, such as Facebook or LinkedIn, allow individuals not only to make contact and stay in touch without ever seeing or talking to each other in person, but they also provide the opportunity to access or visualize the connections of one's contacts. Such platforms provide insights into individual relational environments at a level of breathtaking detail. Using a multilevel evolutionary framework, a theoretical study (Larson, 2016) explored the implications that this informational overdose of insights into social networks may have on gossiping and cooperation. Its main conclusion is surprising and also somewhat disconcerting: highly accurate knowledge of a group's network structure actually may decrease the fitness of a group. Where every individual's position in the network is common knowledge, it is easy to identify and target those in peripheral positions. This makes them easier targets for noncooperative strategies, because due to their weak embeddedness, their capacity to spread gossip, damage reputations, and instigate sanctions is limited. In contrast, where insight into a network is blurry, the opportunities to single out and exploit marginal members are much more limited. Our knowledge of the ability to identify everyone's network position "creates incentives to behave uncooperatively" (Larson, 2016) toward those in the periphery of the network. In fact, where selection pressure at the group level is strong, it is those groups whose members have relatively little accurate knowledge about the network who have an evolutionary advantage – and not groups in which everyone has detailed insights into everybody else's networks. The overall conclusion suggests that the cognitive limitations with regard to our ability to correctly trace our social networks may be the product of natural selection, and that the related errors we make in doing so (e.g., forgetting existing links or adding nonexisting new links) would contribute to facilitate cooperation. From a goal framing perspective, the plain availability of accurate insights into a network structure would increase the saliency of the gain goal and lead individuals to exploit the vulnerable members.

Network scholars studying real-life organizational behavior have found that a more accurate insight into the (power structure) of the informal web of relationships indeed confers individual benefits (Krackhardt, 1990), though it should be stressed that this outcome need not necessarily be the result of exploiting the weak. But in many settings and situations such an unbridled gain goal frame in which individuals systematically exploit the availability of full information about everyone's networks would be highly unlikely. According to this reading, one would expect that the prevalence of this behavior depends on the kind of institutional constraints and the degree to which they support or temper the gain goal frame. For example, where cultural beliefs feature normative obligations toward treating ingroup members fairly, access to accurate knowledge about the group's network structure should be far less likely to result in the exploitation of the less well connected.

5.2 Reputation without Gossip

In teams, groups, and communities, face-to-face interaction offers the opportunity to find out about false information, settle disputes, but also to discard information if coming from a disreputable or untrustworthy source. Even more important, individuals decide what to report and how (Giardini & Wittek, 2019a; Giardini et al., 2019), and this decision is based on the network of relationships they are embedded in and on their knowledge about those relationships (Giardini & Wittek, 2019b; Takacs et al., 2021). This contextual knowledge plays a major role in determining whether and how to gossip (Ellwardt, 2019; see Section 3) and in shaping reputations (Gross & De Dreu, 2019), but it is not the case in the online world. Some differences between offline reputation and its online counterpart are self-evident, such as anonymity, distance, and the scope of the potential audience, whereas some other aspects are less obvious but equally important.

Technology offers opportunities to form, change, and disseminate reputations in ways that are completely different from the past, and we argue that this can have consequences on the motivation to gossip and on the sustainability of cooperation. If gossip is seldom based on a normative goal frame, but rather motivated by a hedonic or a gain goal frame, then reputation effects cannot support cooperation. We will now focus on the differences between online and offline reputation systems in general, before going into online transactions.

In general, the process of reputation building is entirely different in the digital world. Usually, reputations are built on a blend of direct observations and reported evaluations whose validity and reliability can change over time (Giardini et al. 2021). An individual's willingness to accept information coming from others depends on the reliability of the source, but also on the relationships between the three actors in the gossip triad (sender-gossip-receiver) (Giardini & Wittek, 2019a). If an acquaintance tells me that a good friend did something bad, I will be inclined to a suspension of judgment and, at the same time, I will likely refrain from spreading the negative gossip any further. In the offline world, reputation is multidimensional; therefore, its change can take time because different kinds of evidence need to converge. This makes the content of reputational judgments less susceptible to fluctuations, with the result that reliability of the information and trustworthiness of the sender increase. In contrast, in online reputation systems there is no social interaction process related to the transmission of information, but reputations result from algorithms' aggregation of unidimensional assessments. This makes it impossible to distinguish, for instance, between malevolent intentions and innocent mistakes, and the design of the algorithm can determine the final reputation and ranking more than the actual content. In such a setting, a normative goal frame can be hardly sustained because the huge amount of information available and the lack of control over the dissemination process make it unlikely that the information will create any value. On the contrary, hedonic motivations can explain hate speech and clickbait online, therefore leading to disruptive gossip (intended as malicious, aggressive, and not necessarily true information about others).

Social media introduced another major change in the process of reputation formation that makes people's opinions and behaviors immediately and globally available. Unlike gossip in which the third party or target is absent, on social media everybody can disseminate private information about both third parties, and themselves. This opens opportunities for strategic impression and reputation-management and the related potential benefits that may come with it, thereby increasing the salience of the hedonic and/or the gain goal frame.

Another completely new element is that digital traces of someone's opinions or choices are potentially available forever, meaning that reputational damages can occur years after the person exhibited a reprehensible behavior. This creates a cognitive environment that is completely different from the one in which gossip and reputation evolved, characterized by privacy, trust, and the possibility to deny accusations of gossip. Online platforms seem better at supporting hedonic (venting emotions, feeling powerful and recognized, taking revenge) and gain frames (gaining visibility, selling contents to followers, acquiring status as an influencer), while making normative frames barely present.

5.3 Reputation in Online Markets

An interesting consequence of the World Wide Web is the creation of online markets in which anonymous strangers can exchange goods and services without centralized punishment systems. Online reputations are pivotal to establishing trust and trustworthy transactions, but the lack of gossip makes online markets completely different from past markets regulated by gossip and reputation, such as the Maghribi traders (Greif, 1989), or traders in the Champagne fairs (Diekman & Przepiorka, 2019; Milgrom et al., 1990). Gossip requires intimacy and some sort of common ground, but also being embedded in the same group or network, a situation that is clearly different from anonymous reputation scores or reviews. Unlike small and consolidated groups of merchants exchanging one type of product and bound by shared identities, online markets allow the exchange of any kinds of goods and services, legally or not, among complete strangers (Przepiorka et al., 2017). The costs of providing information about products in the online world, as well as the costs of acquiring this information, are very small, therefore providing the ideal situation for reputation systems to work. Honest reviews supposedly offer useful and reliable indications that are essential to build trust between users (Diekman & Przepiorka, 2019), but they also offer a competitive advantage because service or product providers with positive reviews or rankings are selected more often and receive a "reputation premium" (Diekman et al., 2014). Snijders and Matzat (2019) show that the threat of reputation damage is more effective than the promises of building up a positive reputation, and they suggest that it is the mere presence of a reputation system, more than its actual functioning, that supports cooperative exchanges. However, providing reviews is a costly action with no immediate benefits, and the hedonic frame seems to be the main motivation behind them. As studies of online reviews show, the distribution of reviews is usually skewed: the majority of reviews are at the positive end of the rating scale, a few reviews are in the mid-range, and some reviews are at the negative end of the scale (Hu et al., 2017; Moe & Schweidel, 2012). Positive reviews are explained by self-selection of customers who are already positively inclined toward the product and, in terms of goal frames, derive some immediate hedonic satisfaction by publicly praising the product. But online reputation systems are also designed to increase the number of reviews by providing reputational incentives to contributors (for instance, with labels such as "super reviewer" or badge of honor for very prolific reviewers). Reviews written in a gain goal frame are less conducive to sustainable cooperation, as demonstrated by the growing number of studies reporting the many different ways in which reputation systems can be gamed by users who want to gain visibility or downplay competitors (Luca & Zervas, 2016). Companies can pay people to write false reviews (crowdturfing: https://aisel.aisnet.org/ecis2017_rp/124/), and newspapers are now regularly reporting about places and services (such as restaurants) that, even if completely fake and nonexistent, received positive reviews and managed to gain positive reputations.

Observational studies with real reviews point to the multiplicity of factors affecting consumers' choices and reviews (Babic Rosario et al., 2016), but there are few empirical studies investigating ranking behaviors in a controlled way. Capraro et al. (2016) conducted an online empirical study on rankings among players in an online economic game, showing that the evaluation in the form of 1, 3, or 5 stars is not necessarily based on others' actual behaviors, but it is conditional on the reviewer's move in the game. When players could rate other players they encountered in a previous dictator-game, cheaters (i.e., players who chose to defect in the dictator game) gave more positive ratings to other cheaters (in the absence of direct and indirect reciprocity), but they also gave negative rankings to cooperators. Although limited, this evidence suggests that online rankings could be far less objective than previously thought, with important consequences for the reliability of digital assessments.

5.4 The Limits of Quantifying Everything

The principle underlying recommendation systems and rankings is that, given a certain behavior or performance, it is possible to assess it in a measurable way, based on some quantitative indicators. The hidden assumption is that pooling individual information, or the "wisdom of the crowd," can overcome the limitations of individual decision-making (Kameda et al., 2022), or the biases that even experts face when assessing products or outcomes. Regardless of their limitations, the benefits of online rankings and metrics still outweigh their costs (Dellarocas, 2003; Tadelis, 2016), because the numerical indicators of actors' past transactions can enable trustworthy exchanges among complete strangers. If a hedonic and a gain frame can explain online reviews and rankings, the question is whether these same frames can be invoked to understand how rankings and evaluation systems not based on gossip are created.

For example, Global University Rankings were designed to create trusted and objective measures of universities' performance across the world. The Times Higher Education (THE) ranking "has been providing trusted performance data on universities for students and their families, academics, university leaders, governments and industry, since 2004" (www.timeshighereducation.com/world-university-rankings). This and other rankings have created and reinforced the notion that there is a global market on which universities compete and this can be expressed in a single "league table" (Marginson & van der Wende, 2007) for comparative purposes. However, this comparison is biased. Global comparisons are made in relation to one model of institution: the comprehensive research-intensive universities that are more common and established in the Western world. The way in which these "objective" measures of performance are established is also questionable, with metrics measuring prestige but not necessarily the quality of education or the amount of support provided to students. Why should the presence of Nobel Prize winners be an indication of the quality of a higher education institution, when the average age of Nobel Prize winners is around sixty-five and older (www.bbc.com/news/science-environment-37578899), meaning that they are already or about to become retired, with probably few teaching hours and very little engagement in their home universities' policies or decisions? Many Nobel Prize winners built their careers and developed the groundbreaking theories and methods for which they are rewarded when they were probably working somewhere else, so what is the rationale for using the awards they won as an indication of the quality of their current employer?

Another problem of quantification is its application to domains in which they create unintended negative effects. For instance, publishing information about quality rankings of physicians, introduced to improve treatment quality, resulted in a higher number of sick patients not admitted in hospitals, because sick patients are more likely to negatively affect the physicians' scores (Werner & Asch 2005). An interesting analysis of rankings is offered by Esposito and Stark (2019), who frame the contribution of ratings as providing an orientation about what others observe. In their analysis, Esposito and Stark identify four reasons why rankings can be problematic: they simplify too much, they are not transparent, they are not reliable for forecasting, and they are not objective. However, the purpose of rankings is not to provide fully reliable information about reality, but rather to offer a frame of reference to reduce uncertainty: "The success and ability of rankings to act as a reference do not depend, as the order of pre-modern societies, on the claim to correctly describe the world" (p. 19). This analysis of ratings and rankings as contemporary alternatives to gossip-based reputation suggests that being in a normative goal frame when evaluating others can be crucial to sustain cooperation, but this frame is not supported by the current design of reputation systems.

5.5 Conclusions

Our analysis shows that: (1) having a reputation which is not built on gossip (as it is the case with rankings, online and offline) leads to a complete detachment of the content from the process; (2) using assessments based on quantity (number of likes, average review score, etc.) instead of quality reduces the importance of experts and of accreditation and certification systems, with undesired consequences on cooperation. The gradual establishment of the World Wide Web as a new technological environment has not only created an unprecedented range of new communication opportunities, but it has also fundamentally altered the information landscape. Research has only just started to keep track of the implications that these innovations might have for gossip and reputation as tools to sustain cooperation. Overall, the reviewed theories and illustrations suggest two preliminary conclusions concerning the role of new digital environments.

First, several of the explanatory mechanisms that were documented for the offline world seem to replicate also in online environments. Second, some features of digital environments may make it more difficult to sustain cooperation. This holds for those platforms that amplify exposure and reactions to moral outrage, two hedonic motivations that can easily unleash spirals of escalation. And it holds for platforms that provide detection of weakly embedded and therefore less protected individuals.

6 A Research Agenda for Goal Framing Theory, Gossip, and Reputation Effects

Much progress has been made in unraveling the puzzle of sustainable cooperation, and in particular the role that gossip and reputation play in this equation. But as our analysis has made clear, current research finds itself at a crossroads. On the one hand, the economic standard model that still dominates research in this field needs serious revision. This model is unable to account for many of the patterns observed in the empirical literature. On the other hand, the proliferation of social-psychological mini-theories and their application to gossip result in an increasing fragmentation, with the theoretical scope of single studies being limited to the statistical effects investigated in the particular research. This *effectology* is detrimental to cumulative knowledge development about the proximate causes of gossip. Middle-range theorizing that is systematically anchored in an evolutionary approach provides a more fruitful point of departure. The GFT of gossip and reputation elaborated in the previous sections represents such an attempt. It offers an integrative framework that also allows reconciling many of the contradicting findings of previous studies. We conclude by pointing to several potential implications for a future research agenda.

6.1 Beyond the Standard Account

One of the major shortcomings of current theorizing on the gossip-reputation-cooperation triangle is its underdeveloped behavioral microfoundation, in which individuals are either selfish gain seekers or inherently prosocial cooperators. Drawing on evolutionary insights about human-motivated cognition, GFT's model of shifting saliences specifies the conditions under which specific mindsets become dominant. This perspective therefore allows uncovering and correcting the hidden assumptions in economic and game theory's "standard" account, according to which individuals cooperate because they want to avoid getting a bad reputation (rather than because they feel a normative obligation to do so). That is: it is the threat of being gossiped about that keeps people in line. And they want to avoid a bad reputation because others will otherwise not cooperate with them (Gintis & Fehr, 2012; Raub & Weesie, 1990). According to this account, reputation is simply "a characteristic or attribute ascribed" to others by their exchange partners (Raub & Weesie, 1990, p. 629). This characterization neglects that a reputation in the moral domain (as opposed to the domain of competence) always is a socially acquired *evaluative* opinion about an actor's presumed *tendency* to act in a way that can be considered as good or bad according to some mutually agreed standard. Shared norms therefore are a prerequisite for reputation effects (Lindenberg et al., 2020, p. 5).

From a goal framing perspective, the standard account's assumed causal links in the gossip-reputation-cooperation triangle need to be explicated as follows (see Figure 1): (1) Individuals make inferences about third parties' cooperative or noncooperative tendencies (i.e., their intention to comply or violate a norm); (2) Individuals share this evaluation honestly and reliably with others; (3) The resulting reputation will be used by others to cooperate or not cooperate with the third party; (4) The third party anticipates potential negative reputation effects and therefore cooperates.

This perspective acknowledges the crucial role of gossip for the evolution of cooperation, since it simultaneously fosters two ways of adaptation to the environment: control (influencing or shaping the environment in ways that benefit the organism) and prediction (anticipating how the environment will behave). Reputations are prediction devices, but the desire (or need) not to get a bad reputation also has a disciplining effect.

Our goal framing explanation also clearly delimits the scope of the standard account. It suggests that gossip will have reputation effects only under quite specific circumstances. And as we outlined in this Element, these conditions will often not be met. The strongest motives to engage in gossip conversations are hedonic in nature: showing one's virtuousness, taking revenge, bonding, soliciting emotional support, satisfying one's curiosity, venting. Such exchanges are unlikely to result in reputation effects on cooperation, because hedonic motivations will compromise reliability and honesty of the shared information, and it will temper an individual's willingness to incur the costs that would come with active sanctioning. More generally, the goal framing perspective developed here suggests future research should take a more cautious stance when proposing gossip as a golden key to sustainable cooperation.

6.2 Three Open Questions

We selected three key questions that we hope future research would address as concluding remarks for this section.

First, the question under which individuals prefer *not* to share relevant third-party information still constitutes a blind spot of gossip research. Giardini and Wittek (2019b) offer a theoretical framework in which six different mechanisms explain why, on the basis of the expected consequences for the actors in the gossip triad and the relationships among them, senders should refrain from gossiping. Understanding why gossip does not spread is important, because the lack of gossip can explain why deviant behaviors are not exposed and then not punished. Empirical and observational studies in organizations, where the presence of explicit structures, organizational cultures, and defined situations provides clear boundaries, are needed to test the presence of the six mechanisms and whether affective and task interdependence explain the lack of gossip in organizations.

A second line of inquiry that requires further research regards the conditions under which gossip will *not* lead to reputation effects (Lindenberg et al., 2020, p. 132). GFT suggests that such situations will be far more common than one would expect based on the standard account. The high-profile media reports of so many powerful individuals (e.g., in the film industry) who for years and sometimes even decades could abuse their position to mistreat and damage those depending on them are but one example illustrating the causal chain outlined in our model. On the side of the antecedents there is a high-stakes, project-based setting, such as the US movie industry, in which powerful gatekeepers can make or break individual careers. Structural dependence relations are reinforced by a highly competitive and often male-dominated culture. Such settings will suppress the salience of a normative goal frame in all involved stakeholders. Victims of misbehavior and transgressions may gossip to vent their grievances, with close friends, but rarely with those who are potential competitors in the business. As a result, the reach of gossip will be limited, and so will the reputation effects: the information will stay in a small inner circle and not spread to those with real sanctioning power. This same result can also stem from an alternative process. As an illustration, we could focus on the role of the receivers, who can actively downplay the gossip received because they are in a gain frame in which spreading the gossip further can hinder their careers. Assessing the existence of different paths, their antecedents, and consequences would be extremely important to go beyond the standard model and understand reputation effects – and the lack thereof – in the real world.

Third, current reputation models are incomplete because they rely on competing microfoundations, selectively focusing on single actors of the gossip triad. However, individuals are not always guided solely by self-interest or prosocial motivations (also known as "social preferences"). We need an integrative behavioral theory that can consistently explain (a) under which (context) conditions which motivations govern behavior and its absence, (b) the motives of all three actors in the gossip triad, and (c) the consequences of gossip on reputation and (the decline of) cooperation. Goal framing theory offers a way out because it integrates allegedly competing models of human nature, is inherently dynamic due to the a priori hierarchy of goal frame salience, and because it explicates how changing contexts affect shifts in the salience of different mindsets. As an illustration, we can consider the role of different cultures in pushing different frames in the foreground, but only if they are aligned with existing structures. GFT predicts that cultural belief systems would have limited direct effects on gossip and cooperation, and that the strength of their effect depends on the alignment of specific situational cues with the goal frames prioritized by the cultural belief system. Cross-cultural survey studies could be designed to test the GFT prediction that, for individuals holding collectivist beliefs, strong situational hedonic cues can increase an individual's tendency to gossip in two ways. First, they can push normative concerns that would normally inhibit negative talk about one's ingroup members into the cognitive background. Second, they may exacerbate negative feelings toward outgroups, thereby fostering gossip (most likely negative) about outgroup members. A study investigating the prevalence and justifications of ingroup/outgroup gossip, their content and valence in work settings embedded in individualistic and collectivist cultures could provide a useful test of the validity of goal framing theory in explaining the relationship between gossip, reputation, and cooperation.

We started off on our journey on the evolutionary foundations of gossip and reputation with a quote by Lanz on gossip as a "mechanism through which the organized forces of evil gain access to various departments of human life." We want to conclude it with the words of Dunbar (1996, p. 100): "Without gossip, there would be no society. In short, gossip is what makes human society as we know it possible."

References

Agneessens, F., & Wittek, R. (2012). Where do intra-organizational advice relations come from? The role of informal status and social capital in social exchange. *Social Networks*, *34*(3), 333–345. https://doi.org/10.1016/j.socnet.2011.04.002.

Aiello, J. R., & Kolb, K. J. (1995). Electronic performance monitoring and social context: Impact on productivity and stress. *Journal of Applied Psychology*, *80*, 339–353. https://doi.org/10.1037/0021-9010.80.3.339.

Akande, A., & Odewale, F. (1994). One more time: How to stop company rumours. *Leadership & Organization Development Journal*, *15*(4), 27–30. https://doi.org/10.1108/01437739410059881.

Alexander, R. D. (1987). *The Biology of Moral Systems*. Aldine de Gruyter.

Andreozzi, L., Ploner, M., & Saral, A. S. (2020). The stability of conditional cooperation: Beliefs alone cannot explain the decline of cooperation in social dilemmas. *Scientific Reports*, *10*(1), 13610. https://doi.org/10.1038/s41598-020-70681-z.

Apicella, C. L., & Silk, J. B. (2019). The evolution of human cooperation. *Current Biology*, *29*(11), R447–R450. https://doi.org/10.1016/j.cub.2019.03.036.

Babić Rosario, A., Sotgiu, F., De Valck, K., & Bijmolt, T. H. A. (2016). The effect of electronic word of mouth on sales: A meta-analytic review of platform, product, and metric factors. *Journal of Marketing Research*, *53* (3), 297–318. https://doi.org/10.1509/jmr.14.0380.

Baker, J. S., & Jones, M. A. (1996). The poison grapevine: How destructive are gossip and rumor in the workplace? *Human Resource Development Quarterly*, *7*(1), 75–86. https://doi.org/10.1002/hrdq.3920070108.

Barclay, P. (2016). Biological markets and the effects of partner choice on cooperation and friendship. *Current Opinion in Psychology*, *7*, 33–38. https://doi.org/10.1016/j.copsyc.2015.07.012.

Barclay, P., & Barker, J. L. (2020). Greener than thou: People who protect the environment are more cooperative, compete to be environmental, and benefit from reputation. *Journal of Environmental Psychology*, *72*, 101441. https://doi.org/10.1016/j.jenvp.2020.101441.

Bardsley, N., & Sausgruber, R. (2005). Conformity and reciprocity in public good provision. *Journal of Economic Psychology*, *26*(5), 664–681. https://doi.org/10.1016/j.joep.2005.02.001.

Barkow, J. H. (1992). Beneath new culture is old psychology: Gossip and social stratification. In J. H. Barkow, L. Cosmides, & J. Tooby (Eds.), *The Adapted Mind: Evolutionary Psychology and the Generation of Culture* (pp. 627–637). Oxford University Press.

Bateson, P., & Laland, K. N. (2013). Tinbergen's four questions: An appreciation and an update. *Trends in Ecology & Evolution*, *28*(12), 712–718. https://doi.org/10.1016/j.tree.2013.09.013.

Baumeister, R. F., Zhang, L., & Vohs, K. D. (2004). Gossip as cultural learning. *Review of General Psychology*, *8*(2), 111–121. https://doi.org/10.1037/1089-2680.8.2.111.

Beersma, B., & Van Kleef, G. A. (2012). Why people gossip: An empirical analysis of social motives, antecedents, and consequences. *Journal of Applied Social Psychology*, *42*(11), 2640–2670. https://doi.org/10.1111/j.1559-1816.2012.00956.x.

Beersma, B., Van Kleef, G. A., & Dijkstra, M. T. (2019). Antecedents and consequences of gossip in work groups. In F. Giardini & R. Wittek (Eds.), *The Oxford Handbook of Gossip and Reputation* (pp. 417–434). Oxford University Press.

Ben-Ze'ev, A., & Goodman, R. F. (Eds.). (1994). *Good Gossip*. University Press of Kansas.

Bertolotti, T., & Magnani, L. (2014). An epistemological analysis of gossip and gossip-based knowledge. *Synthese*, *191*(17), 4037–4067. https://doi.org/10.1007/s11229-014-0514-2.

Bicchieri, C. (2017). *Norms in the Wild: How to Diagnose, Measure, and Change Social Norms*. Oxford University Press.

Blau, P. M. (1963). *The Dynamics of Bureaucracy*. Chicago University Press.

Boehm, C. (2019). Gossip and reputation in small-scale societies. In F. Giardini & R. Wittek (Eds.), *The Oxford Handbook of Gossip and Reputation* (pp. 253–274). Oxford University Press. https://doi.org/10.1093/oxfordhb/9780190494087.013.14.

Boero, R. (2019). Neuroscientific methods. In F. Giardini & R. Wittek (Eds.), *The Oxford Handbook of Gossip and Reputation* (pp. 118–131). Oxford University Press. https://doi.org/10.1093/oxfordhb/9780190494087.013.7.

Borgatti, S. P., & Foster, P. C. (2003). The network paradigm in organizational research: A review and typology. *Journal of Management*, *29*(6), 991–1013. https://doi.org/10.1016/S0149-2063_03_00087-4.

Bowles, S., & Gintis, H. (2011). *A Cooperative Species: Human Reciprocity and Its Evolution*. Princeton University Press.

Boyd, D. (2008). Why youth (heart) social network sites: The role of networked publics in teenage social life. In D. Buckingham (Ed.), *Youth, Identity, and Digital* Media (pp. 119–142). The MIT Press.

Boyd, R., & Richerson, P. J. (2006). Solving the puzzle of human cooperation. In S. Levinson & P. Jaisson (Eds.), *Evolution and Culture: A Fyssen Foundation Symposium* (pp. 105–132). The MIT Press.

Brady, W. J., Wills, J. A., Jost, J. T., Tucker, J. A., & Van Bavel, J. J. (2017). Emotion shapes the diffusion of moralized content in social networks. *Proceedings of the National Academy of Sciences*, *114*(28), 7313–7318. https://doi.org/10.1073/pnas.1618923114.

Brady, W., Mclaughlin, K., Doan, T., & Crockett, M. (2021). How social learning amplifies moral outrage expression in online social networks. *Science Advances*, *7*, 15.

Brenneis, D. (1984). Grog and gossip in Bhatgaon: Style and substance in Fiji Indian conversation. *American Ethnologist*, *11*(3), 487–506. https://doi.org/10.1525/ae.1984.11.3.02a00050.

Brison, K. J. (1992). *Just Talk: Gossip, Meetings, and Power in a Papua New Guinea Village*. University of California Press.

Brondino, N., Fusar-Poli, L., & Politi, P. (2017). Something to talk about: Gossip increases oxytocin levels in a near real-life situation. *Psychoneuroendocrinology*, *77*, 218–224. https://doi.org/10.1016/j.psyneuen.2016.12.014.

Burt, R. S. (2001). Bandwidth and echo: Trust, information, and gossip in social networks. In J. Rauch & A. Casella (Eds.), *Networks and Markets* (pp. 30–74). Russell Sage Foundation.

Burt, R. S. (2009). *Structural Holes: The Social Structure of Competition*. Harvard University Press.

Burt, R. S., & Soda, G. (2021). Network capabilities: Brokerage as a bridge between network theory and the resource-based view of the firm. *Journal of Management*, *47*(7), 1698–1719. https://doi.org/10.1177/0149206320988764.

Burton-Chellew, M. N., & West, S. A. (2013). Prosocial preferences do not explain human cooperation in public-goods games. *Proceedings of the National Academy of Sciences of the United States of America*, *110*(1), 216–221. https://doi.org/10.1073/pnas.1210960110.

Burton-Chellew, M. N., Nax, H. H., & West, S. A. (2015). Payoff-based learning explains the decline in cooperation in public goods games. *Proceedings of the Royal Society B: Biological Sciences*, *282*(1801), 20142678. https://doi.org/10.1098/rspb.2014.2678.

Camerer, C. F., & Thaler, R. H. (1995). Anomalies: Ultimatums, dictators and manners. *Journal of Economic Perspectives*, *9*(2), 209–219. https://doi.org/10.1257/jep.9.2.209.

Campbell, A. (2004). Female competition: Causes, constraints, content, and contexts. *Journal of Sex Research*, *41*(1), 16–26. https://doi.org/10.1080/00224490409552210.

Capraro, V., Giardini, F., Vilone, D., & Paolucci, M. (2016). Partner selection supported by opaque reputation promotes cooperative behavior. *Judgment and Decision Making*, *11*(6), 589–600. https://doi.org/10.1017/S1930297500004800.

Carpenter, J. P. (2004). When in Rome: Conformity and the provision of public goods. *The Journal of Socio-Economics*, *33*(4), 395–408. https://doi.org/10.1016/j.socec.2004.04.009.

Chatman, J. A., & Barsade, S. G. (1995). Personality, organizational culture, and cooperation: Evidence from a business simulation. *Administrative Science Quarterly*, *40*, 423–443. https://doi.org/10.2307/2393792.

Chaudhuri, A. (2011). Sustaining cooperation in laboratory public goods experiments: A selective survey of the literature. *Experimental Economics*, *14*(1), 47–83. https://doi.org/10.1007/s10683-010-9257-1.

Chiao, J. Y., & Blizinsky, K. D. (2010). Culture–gene coevolution of individualism–collectivism and the serotonin transporter gene. *Proceedings of the Royal Society B: Biological Sciences*, *277*(1681), 529–537. https://doi.org/10.1098/rspb.2009.1650.

Choi, I., & Nisbett, R. E. (1998). Situational salience and cultural differences in the correspondence bias and actor-observer bias. *Personality and Social Psychology Bulletin*, *24*(9), 949–960. https://doi.org/10.1177/0146167298249003.

Coleman, J. S. (1990). *Foundations of Social Theory*. Harvard University Press.

Cowden, C. C. (2012) Game Theory, Evolutionary Stable Strategies and the Evolution of Biological Interactions. *Nature Education Knowledge*, *3*(10), 6. www.nature.com/scitable/knowledge/library/game-theory-evolutionary-stable-strategies-and-the-25953132/.

Crockett, M. J. (2017). Moral outrage in the digital age. *Nature Human Behaviour* *1*(11), 769–771. https://doi.org/10.1038/s41562-017-0213-3.

Dana, J., Weber, R. A., & Kuang, J. X. (2007). Exploiting moral wiggle room: Experiments demonstrating an illusory preference for fairness. *Economic Theory*, *33*(1), 67–80. www.jstor.org/stable/27822583.

Davidson, R., & Henderson, R. (2000). Electronic performance monitoring: A laboratory investigation of the influence of monitoring and difficulty on task performance, mood state, and self-reported stress levels. *Journal of*

Applied Social Psychology, *30*(5), 906–920. https://doi.org/10.1111/j.1559-1816.2000.tb02502.x.

Davis, A., Vaillancourt, T., Arnocky, S., & Doyel, R. (2019). Women's gossip as an intrasexual competition strategy. In F. Giardini & R. Wittek (Eds.), *The Oxford Handbook of Gossip and Reputation* (pp. 303–321). Oxford University Press. https://doi.org/10.1093/oxfordhb/9780190494087.013.16.

De Backer, C. (2005). Like Belgian chocolate for the universal mind: Interpersonal and media gossip from an evolutionary perspective. Unpublished doctoral dissertation. Ghent: Ghent University, Belgium.

De Clercq, D. (2022). Exposure to workplace bullying and negative gossip behaviors: Buffering roles of personal and contextual resources. *Business Ethics, the Environment & Responsibility*, *31*(3), 859–874. https://doi.org/10.1111/beer.12436.

De Clercq, D., Haq, I. U., & Azeem, M. U. (2019). Gossiping about outsiders: How time-related work stress among collectivistic employees hinders job performance. *Journal of Management & Organization*, *29*(2), 1–16. https://doi.org/10.1017/jmo.2019.56.

Dellarocas, C. (2003). The digitization of word of mouth: Promise and challenges of online feedback mechanisms. *Management Science*, *49*(10), 1407–1424. https://doi.org/10.1287/mnsc.49.10.1407.17308.

Den Bak, I. M., & Ross, H. S. (1996). I'm telling! The content, context, and consequences of children's tattling on their siblings. *Social Development*, *5* (3), 292–309. https://doi.org/10.1111/j.1467-9507.1996.tb00087.x.

Diekmann, A., & Przepiorka, W. (2019). Trust and reputation in markets. In F. Giardini & R. Wittek (Eds.), *The Oxford Handbook of Gossip and Reputation* (pp. 383–400). Oxford University Press. https://doi.org/10.1093/oxfordhb/9780190494087.013.20.

Diekmann, A., Jann, B., Przepiorka, W., & Wehrli, S. (2014). Reputation formation and the evolution of cooperation in anonymous online markets. *American Sociological Review*, *79*(1), 65–85. https://doi.org/10.1177/0003122413512316.

Do Canto, N. R., Grunert, K. G., & Dutra de Barcellos, M. (2023). Goal-framing theory in environmental behaviours: Review, future research agenda and possible applications in behavioural change. *Journal of Social Marketing*, *13*(1), 20–40. https://doi.org/10.1108/JSOCM-03-2021-0058.

Dores Cruz, T. D., Nieper, A. S., Testori, M., Martinescu, E., & Beersma, B. (2021). An integrative definition and framework to study gossip. *Group &*

Organization Management, *46*(2), 252–285. https://doi.org/10.31234/osf.io/b8x57.

Dores Cruz, T. D., Thielmann, I., Columbus, S., et al. (2021). Gossip and reputation in everyday life. *Philosophical Transactions of the Royal Society B*, *376*(1838), 20200301. https://doi.org/10.1098/rstb.2020.0301.

Duca, S., & Nax, H. H. (2018). Groups and scores: The decline of cooperation. *Journal of the Royal Society Interface*, *15*(144), 20180158. https://doi.org/10.1098/rsif.2018.0158.

Dunbar, R. I. (1997). Groups, gossip, and the evolution of language. In: Schmitt, A., Atzwanger, K., Grammer, K., Schäfer, K. (eds) New Aspects of Human Ethology. Springer, Boston, MA (pp. 77–89). https://doi.org/10.1007/978-0-585-34289-4_5

Dunbar, R. I. (2004). Gossip in evolutionary perspective. *Review of General Psychology*, *8*(2), 100–110. https://doi.org/10.1037/1089-2680.8.2.100.

Dunbar, R. I. (2009). The social brain hypothesis and its implications for social evolution. *Annals of Human Biology*, *36*(5), 562–572. https://doi.org/10.1080/03014460902960289.

Dunbar, R. I. M., Marriott, A., & Duncan, N. D. C. (1997). Human conversational behavior. *Human Nature*, *8*(3), 231–246. https://doi.org/10.1007/BF02912493.

Dunbar, R. I. (1996). *Grooming, Gossip and the Evolution of Language*. Harvard University Press.

Eckert, P. (1990). Cooperative competition in adolescent "girl talk." *Discourse Processes*, *13*(1), 91–122. https://doi.org/10.1080/01638539009544748.

Eder, D., & Enke, J. L. (1991). The structure of gossip: Opportunities and constraints on collective expression among adolescents. *American Sociological Review*, *56*(4), 494–508. https://doi.org/10.2307/2096270.

Elias, N., & Scotson, J. L. (1994). *The Established and the Outsiders*. Sage.

Ellickson, R. C. (1991). *Order without Law: How Neighbors Settle Disputes*. Harvard University Press.

Ellwardt, L. (2019). Gossip and reputation in social networks. In F. Giardini & R. Wittek (Eds.), *The Oxford Handbook of Gossip and Reputation* (pp. 435–457). Oxford University Press. https://doi.org/10.1093/oxfordhb/9780190494087.013.23.

Ellwardt, L., Steglich, C., & Wittek, R. (2012). The co-evolution of gossip and friendship in workplace social networks. *Social Networks*, *34*(4), 623–633. https://doi.org/10.1016/j.socnet.2012.07.002.

Emerson, R. M. (1962). Power-dependence relations. *American Sociological Review*, *27*, 31–41. https://doi.org/10.2307/2089716.

Emler, N. (1994). Gossip, reputation, and social adaptation. In R. F. Goodman & A. Ben-Ze'ev (Eds.), *Good Gossip* (pp. 117–138). Kansas University Press.

Emler, N. (2019). Human sociality and psychological foundations. In F. Giardini & R. Wittek (Eds.), *The Oxford Handbook of Gossip and Reputation* (pp. 47–68). Oxford University Press. https://doi.org/10.1093/oxfordhb/9780190494087.013.3.

Engelmann, J. M., Herrmann, E., & Tomasello, M. (2016). Preschoolers affect others' reputations through prosocial gossip. *British Journal of Developmental Psychology*, *34*(3), 447–460. https://doi.org/10.1111/bjdp.12143.

Eriksson, K., Strimling, P., Gelfand, M., et al. (2021). Perceptions of the appropriate response to norm violation in 57 societies. *Nature Communications*, *12*(1), 1481. https://doi.org/10.1038/s41467-021-21602-9.

Esposito, E., & Stark, D. (2019). What's observed in a rating? Rankings as orientation in the face of uncertainty. *Theory, Culture & Society*, *36*(4), 3–26. https://doi-org.proxy-ub.rug.nl/10.1177/0263276419826276.

Etienne, J. (2011). Compliance theory: A goal framing approach. *Law & Policy*, *33*(3), 305–333. https://doi.org/10.1111/j.1467-9930.2011.00340.x.

Fehr, D., & Sutter, M. (2019). Gossip and the efficiency of interactions. *Games and Economic Behavior*, *113*, 448–460. https://doi.org/10.1016/j.geb.2018.10.003.

Feinberg, M., Willer, R., Stellar, J., & Keltner, D. (2012). The virtues of gossip: Reputational information sharing as prosocial behavior. *Journal of Personality and Social Psychology*, *102*(5), 1015. https://doi.org/10.1037/a0026650.

Fine, G. A., & Rosnow, R. L. (1978). Gossip, gossipers, gossiping. *Personality and Social Psychology Bulletin*, *4*(1), 161–168. https://doi.org/10.1177/014616727800400135.

Flaxman, S., Goel, S., & Rao, J. M. (2016). Filter bubbles, echo chambers, and online news consumption. *Public Opinion Quarterly*, *80*(S1), 298–320. https://doi.org/10.1093/poq/nfw006.

Fonseca, M. A., & Peters, K. (2018). Will any gossip do? Gossip does not need to be perfectly accurate to promote trust. *Games and Economic Behavior*, *107*, 253–281. https://doi.org/10.1016/j.geb.2017.09.015.

Fosgaard, T. R. (2018). Cooperation stability: A representative sample in the lab. IFRO Working Paper No. 2018/08. University of Copenhagen, Department of Food and Resource Economics (IFRO), Copenhagen. https://EconPapers.repec.org/RePEc:foi:wpaper:2018_08.

Foster, E. K. (2004). Research on gossip: Taxonomy, methods, and future directions. *Review of General Psychology, 8*(2), 78–99. https://doi.org/10.1037/1089-2680.8.2.78.

French, J. R., Raven, B., & Cartwright, D. (1959). The bases of social power. *Classics of Organization Theory, 7*, 311–320.

Fu, F., Hauert, C., Nowak, M. A., & Wang, L. (2008). Reputation-based partner choice promotes cooperation in social networks. *Physical Review E, 78*(2), 026117. https://doi.org/10.1103/PhysRevE.78.026117.

Gabriels, K., & De Backer, C. J. (2016). Virtual gossip: How gossip regulates moral life in virtual worlds. *Computers in Human Behavior, 63*, 683–693. https://doi.org/10.1016/j.chb.2016.05.065.

Gambetta, D. (1994). Godfather's gossip. *European Journal of Sociology/ Archives Européennes de Sociologie, 35*(2), 199–223. https://doi.org/10.1017/S0003975600006846.

Garfield, Z. H., Schacht, R., Post, E. R., et al. (2021). The content and structure of reputation domains across human societies: A view from the evolutionary social sciences. *Philosophical Transactions of the Royal Society B, 376* (1838), 20200296. https://doi.org/10.1098/rstb.2020.0296.

Gelfand, M. J., & Lun, J. (2013). The culture of the situation: The role of situational strength in cultural systems: Situational constraint. *Asian Journal of Social Psychology, 16*(1), 34–38. https://doi.org/10.1111/ajsp.12018.

Giardini, F. (2012). Deterrence and transmission as mechanisms ensuring reliability of gossip. *Cognitive Processing, 13*, 465–475. https://doi.org/10.1007/s10339-011-0421-0.

Giardini, F., & Wittek, R. (2019a). Gossip, reputation and sustainable cooperation: Sociological foundations. In F. Giardini & R. Wittek (Eds.), *The Oxford Handbook of Gossip and Reputation* (pp. 23–46). Oxford University Press. https://doi.org/10.1093/oxfordhb/9780190494087.013.2.

Giardini, F., & Wittek, R. P. M. (2019b). Silence is golden. Six reasons inhibiting the spread of third-party gossip. *Frontiers in Psychology, 10*, 1120. https://doi.org/10.3389/fpsyg.2019.01120.

Giardini, F., Balliet, D., Power, E. A., Számadó, S., & Takács, K. (2022). Four puzzles of reputation-based cooperation. *Human Nature, 33*(1), 43–61. https://doi.org/10.1007/s12110-021-09419-3.

Giardini, F., Fitneva, S. A., & Tamm, A. (2019). "Someone told me": Preemptive reputation protection in communication. *PloS One, 14*(4), e0200883. https://doi.org/10.1371/journal.pone.0200883.

Giardini, F., Vilone, D., Sánchez, A., & Antonioni, A. (2021). Gossip and competitive altruism support cooperation in a Public Good game. *Philosophical Transactions of the Royal Society B, 376*(1838), 20200303.

Gigerenzer, G., & Gaissmaier, W. (2011). Heuristic decision making. *Annual Review of Psychology, 62*, 451–482. https://doi.org/10.1146/annurev-psych-120709-145346.

Gintis, H. (2016). Homo Ludens: Social rationality and political behavior. *Journal of Economic Behavior & Organization, 126*, 95–109. https://doi.org/10.1016/j.jebo.2016.01.004.

Gintis, H., & Fehr, E. (2012). The social structure of cooperation and punishment. *Behavioral and Brain Science, 35*(1), 28–29. https://doi.org/10.1017/S0140525X11000914.

Gluckman, M. (1963). Papers in honor of Melville J. Herskovits: Gossip and scandal. *Current Anthropology, 4*(3), 307–316.

Gluckman, M. (1968). Psychological, sociological and anthropological explanations of witchcraft and gossip: A clarification. *Man, 3*(1), 20–34. https://doi.org/10.2307/2799409.

Goffman, E. (1949). Presentation of self in everyday life. *American Journal of Sociology, 55*, 6–7.

Goldstein, D. G., & Gigerenzer, G. (2002). Models of ecological rationality: The recognition heuristic. *Psychological Review, 109*(1), 75–90. https://doi.org/10.1037/0033-295X.109.1.75.

Goodman, R. F., & Ben-Ze'ev, A. (Eds.) (1994). *Good Gossip*. University Press of Kansas.

Gottman, J. M., & Mettetal, G. (1986). Speculations about social and affective development: Friendship and acquaintanceship through adolescence. In J. M. Gottman & J. G. Parker (Eds.), *Conversations of Friends: Speculations on Affective Development* (pp. 192–237). Cambridge University Press.

Greif, A. (1989). Reputation and coalitions in medieval trade: evidence on the Maghribi traders. *The Journal of Economic History, 49*(4), 857–882.

Greif, A. (1994). Cultural beliefs and the organization of society: A historical and theoretical reflection on collectivist and individualist societies. *Journal of Political Economy, 102*(5), 912–950. https://doi.org/10.1086/261959.

Gross, J., & De Dreu, C. K. (2019). The rise and fall of cooperation through reputation and group polarization. *Nature Communications, 10*(1), 1–10. https://doi.org/10.1038/s41467-019-08727-8.

Guala, F. (2012). Reciprocity: Weak or strong? What punishment experiments do (and do not) demonstrate. *Behavioral and Brain Sciences, 35*(1), 1–15. https://doi.org/10.1017/S0140525X11000069.

Hartung, F.-M., Krohn, C., & Pirschtat, M. (2019). Better than its reputation? Gossip and the reasons why we and individuals with "dark" personalities talk about others. *Frontiers in Psychology, 10*, 10–16. https://doi.org/10.3389/fpsyg.2019.01162.

Haselton, M. G., Nettle, D., & Murray, D. R. (2015). The evolution of cognitive bias. In D. Buss (Ed.), *The Handbook of Evolutionary Psychology* (724–746). Wiley.

Hauser, D. J., Nowak, M. A., & Rand, D. G. (2014). Punishment does not promote cooperation under exploration dynamics when anti-social punishment is possible. *Journal of Theoretical Biology, 360*, 163–171. https://doi.org/10.1016/j.jtbi.2014.06.041.

Haux, L., Engelmann, J. M., Herrmann, E., & Tomasello, M. (2017). Do young children preferentially trust gossip or firsthand observation in choosing a collaborative partner? *Social Development, 26*(3), 466–474. https://doi.org/10.1111/sode.12225.

Heine, S. J. (2010). Cultural psychology. In S. T. Fiske, D. T. Gilbert, & G. Lindzey (Eds.), *Handbook of Social Psychology* (pp. 1423–1464). Wiley. https://doi.org/10.1002/9780470561119.socpsy002037.

Heintz, C., Celse, J., Giardini, F., & Max, S. (2015). Facing expectations: Those that we prefer to fulfil and those that we disregard. *Judgment & Decision Making, 10*(5), 442–445. https://doi.org/10.1017/S1930297500005581.

Hess, N. H., & Hagen, E. H. (2019). Gossip, reputation, and friendship in within-group competition. In F. Giardini & R. Wittek (Eds.), *The Oxford Handbook of Gossip and Reputation* (pp. 275–302). Oxford University Press. https://doi.org/10.1093/oxfordhb/9780190494087.013.15.

Hess, N. H., & Hagen, E. H. (2021). Competitive gossip: The impact of domain, resource value, resource scarcity and coalitions. *Philosophical Transactions of the Royal Society B, 376*(1838), 20200305. https://doi.org/10.1098/rstb.2020.0305.

House, B. R., Kanngiesser, P., Barrett, H. C. et al. (2020). Universal norm psychology leads to societal diversity in prosocial behaviour and development. *Nature Human Behaviour, 4*(1), 36–44.

Hruschka, D. J., & Henrich, J. (2013). Institutions, parasites and the persistence of ingroup preferences. *PLoS One, 8*(5), e63642. https://doi.org/10.1371/journal.pone.0063642.

Hu, N., Pavlou, P. A., & Zhang, J. (2017). On self-selection biases in online product reviews. *MIS Quarterly, 41*(2), 449–475. www.jstor.org/stable/26629722.

Huff, L., & Kelley, L. (2003). Levels of organizational trust in individualist versus collectivist societies: A seven-nation study. *Organization Science, 14*(1), 81–90. https://doi.org/10.1287/orsc.14.1.81.12807.

Ingram, G. P. (2019). Gossip and reputation in childhood. In F. Giardini & R. Wittek (Eds.), *The Oxford Handbook of Gossip and Reputation* (pp.

131–151). Oxford University Press. https://doi.org/10.1093/oxfordhb/9780190494087.013.8.

Izuma, K. (2012). The social neuroscience of reputation. *Neuroscience Research*, *72*(4), 283–288. https://doi.org/10.1016/j.neures.2012.01.003.

Jeuken, E., Beersma, B., ten Velden, F. S., & Dijkstra, M. T. (2015). Aggression as a motive for gossip during conflict: The role of power, social value orientation, and counterpart's behavior. *Negotiation and Conflict Management Research*, *8* (3), 137–152. https://doi.org/10.1111/ncmr.12053.

Jones, G. M., Schieffelin, B. B., & Smith, R. E. (2011). When friends who talk together stalk together: Online gossip as metacommunication. In C. Thurlow & K. Mroczek (Eds.), *Digital Discourse: Language in the New Media* (pp. 26–47). Oxford University Press. https://doi.org/10.1093/acprof:oso/9780199795437.003.0002.

Kahneman, D., & Tversky, A. (2013). Prospect theory: An analysis of decision under risk. In L. MacLean & W. Ziemba (Eds.),*Handbook of the Fundamentals of Financial Decision Making: Part I* (pp. 99–127). World Scientific. https://doi.org/10.1142/8557.

Kahneman, D., Knetsch, J. L., & Thaler, R. H. (1991). Anomalies: The endowment effect, loss aversion, and status quo bias. *Journal of Economic Perspectives*, *5*(1), 193–206. https://doi.org/10.1257/jep.5.1.193.

Kameda, T., Toyokawa, W., & Tindale, R. S. (2022). Information aggregation and collective intelligence beyond the wisdom of crowds. *Nature Reviews Psychology*, *1*(6), 345–357. https://doi.org/10.1038/s44159-022-00054-y.

Keizer, K., Lindenberg, S., & Steg, L. (2008). The spreading of disorder. *Science*, *322*(5908), 1681–1685. https://doi.org/10.1126/science.11614.

Keltner, D., & Haidt, J. (1999). Social functions of emotions at four levels of analysis. *Cognition & Emotion*, *13*(5), 505–521. https://doi.org/10.1080/026999399379168.

Kniffin, K. M., & Wilson, D. S. (2005). Utilities of gossip across organizational levels: Multilevel selection, free-riders, and teams. *Human Nature*, *16*(3), 278–292. https://doi.org/10.1007/s12110-005-1011-6.

Kniffin, K. M., & Sloan Wilson, D. (2010). Evolutionary perspectives on workplace gossip: Why and how gossip can serve groups. *Group & Organization Management*, *35*(2), 150–176. https://doi.org/10.1177/1059601109360390.

Knoch, D., Schneider, F., Schunk, D., Hohmann, M., & Fehr, E. (2009). Disrupting the prefrontal cortex diminishes the human ability to build a good reputation. *Proceedings of the National Academy of Sciences*, *106* (49), 20895–20899. https://doi.org/10.1073/pnas.0911619106.

Kochanska, G. (2002), Committed compliance, moral self, and internalization: A mediational model. *Developmental Psychology, 38*, 339–351. https://doi.org/10.1037/0012-1649.38.3.339.

Kock, N. (2004). The psychobiological model: Towards a new theory of computer-mediated communication based on Darwinian evolution. *Organization Science, 15*(3), 327–348. https://doi.org/10.1287/orsc.1040.0071.

Krackhardt, D. (1990). Assessing the political landscape: Structure, cognition, and power in organizations. *Administrative Science Quarterly, 35*(2), 342–369. https://doi.org/10.2307/2393394.

Kurland, N. B., & Pelled, L. H. (2000). Passing the word: Toward a model of gossip and power in the workplace. *Academy of Management Review, 25*(2), 428–438. https://doi.org/10.5465/amr.2000.3312928.

Kurzban, R., Tooby, J., & Cosmides, L. (2001). Can race be erased? Coalitional computation and social categorization. *Proceedings of the National Academy of Sciences, 98*(26), 15387–15392. https://doi.org/10.1073/pnas.251541498.

Laidre, M. E., Lamb, A., Shultz, S., & Olsen, M. (2013). Making sense of information in noisy networks: Human communication, gossip, and distortion. *Journal of Theoretical Biology, 317*, 152–160. https://doi.org/10.1016/j.jtbi.2012.09.009.

Lanz, H. (1936). Metaphysics of Gossip. *International Journal of Ethics, 46*(4), 492–499. https://doi.org/10.1086/intejethi.46.4.2989287.

Larson, J. M. (2016). The evolutionary advantage of limited network knowledge. *Journal of Theoretical Biology, 398*, 43–51. https://doi.org/10.1016/j.jtbi.2016.03.017.

Ledyard, O. (1995). Public goods: Some experimental results. In H. Kagel & A. Roth (Eds.), *Handbook of Experimental Economics* (pp. 111–194). Princeton University Press.

Lee, S. H., & Barnes, C. M. (2021). An attributional process model of workplace gossip. *Journal of Applied Psychology, 106*(2), 300–316. https://doi.org/10.1037/apl0000504.

Lehmann, J., Korstjens, A. H., & Dunbar, R. I. M. (2007). Group size, grooming and social cohesion in primates. *Animal Behavior, 74*(6), 1617–1629. https://doi.org/10.1016/j.anbehav.2006.10.025.

Leimar, O., & Hammerstein, P. (2001). Evolution of cooperation through indirect reciprocity. *Proceedings of the Royal Society of London. Series B: Biological Sciences, 268*(1468), 745–753. https://doi.org/10.1098/rspb.2000.1573.

Leinfellner, W. (1998). Game theory, sociodynamics, and cultural evolution. In W. Leinfellner & E. Köhler (Eds.), *Game Theory, Experience, Rationality.* Vienna Circle Institute Yearbook [1997], Vol. 5. Springer.

Lindenberg, S. (1981). Rational, repetitive choice: The discrimination model versus the Camilleri–Berger model. *Social Psychology Quarterly, 44*(4), 312–330. https://doi.org/10.2307/3033900.

Lindenberg, S. (1985). An assessment of the new political economy: Its potential for the social sciences and for sociology in particular. *Sociological Theory, 3*(1), 99–114. https://doi.org/10.2307/202177.

Lindenberg, S. (2002). Solidarity, its microfoundations and macrodependence: A framing approach. In O. Favereau & E. Lazega (Eds.), *Conventions and Structures in Economic Organization: Markets, Networks, and Hierarchies* (pp. 282–328). Edward Elgar. https://doi.org/10.4337/9781781952863.

Lindenberg, S. (2015). The third speed: Flexible activation and its link to self-regulation. *Review of Behavioral Economics, 2*, 147–160. http://dx.doi.org/10.1561/105.00000024.

Lindenberg, S. (2023). Social rationality and economic sociology. In M. Zafirovski (Ed.), *The Routledge International Handbook of Economic Sociology* (pp. 247–270). Routledge. http://dx.doi.org/10.4324/9780367817152-15.

Lindenberg, S., & Foss, N. J. (2011). Managing joint production motivation: The role of goal framing and governance mechanisms. *Academy of Management Review, 36*(3), 500–525. https://doi.org/10.5465/amr.2010.0021.

Lindenberg, S., & Steg, L. (2007). Normative, gain and hedonic goal frames guiding environmental behavior. *Journal of Social Issues, 63*(1), 117–137. https://doi.org/10.1111/j.1540-4560.2007.00499.x.

Lindenberg, S., Wittek, R., & Giardini, F. (2020). Reputation effects, embeddedness, and Granovetter's Error. In V. Buskens, R. Corten, & C. Snijders (Eds.), *Advances in the Sociology of Trust and Cooperation: Theory, Experiments, and Field Studies* (pp. 113–140). De Gruyter Oldenbourg.

Luca, M., & Zervas, G. (2016). Fake it till you make it: Reputation, competition, and Yelp review fraud. *Management Science, 62*(12), 3412–3427. https://doi.org/10.1287/mnsc.2015.2304.

Lyons, M. T., & Hughes, S. (2015). Malicious mouths? The Dark Triad and motivations for gossip. *Personality and Individual Differences, 78*, 1–4. https://doi.org/10.1016/j.paid.2015.01.009.

Manesi, Z., Van Lange, P. A., & Pollet, T. V. (2016). Eyes wide open: Only eyes that pay attention promote prosocial behavior. *Evolutionary Psychology, 14* (2), 1–15. https://doi.org/10.1177/1474704916640780.

Manrique, H. M., Zeidler, H., Roberts, G., et al. (2021). The psychological foundations of reputation-based cooperation. *Philosophical Transactions of the Royal Society B, 376*(1838), 1–11. https://doi.org/10.1098/rstb.2020.0287.

Marginson, S., & Van der Wende, M. (2007). To rank or to be ranked: The impact of global rankings in higher education. *Journal of Studies in International Education, 11*(3–4), 306–329. https://doi.org/10.1177/1028315307303544.

Martinescu, E., Janssen, O., & Nijstad, B. A. (2019). Gossip and emotion. In F. Giardini & R. Wittek (Eds.), *The Oxford Handbook of Gossip and Reputation* (pp. 152–169). Oxford University Press. https://doi.org/10.1093/oxfordhb/9780190494087.013.9.

Mascaro, O., & Sperber, D. (2009). The moral, epistemic, and mindreading components of children's vigilance towards deception. *Cognition, 112*(3), 367–380. https://doi.org/10.1016/j.cognition.2009.05.012.

Masum, H., & Tovey, M. (2011). *The Reputation Society: How Online Opinions are Reshaping the Offline World*. MIT Press.

Masum, H., & Zhang, Y. (2004). Manifesto for the reputation society. *First Monday, 9*(7). https://doi.org/10.5210/fm.v9i7.1158.

Mayr, E. (1963). *Animal Species and Evolution*. Harvard University Press.

McAndrew, F. T. (2019). Gossip as a social skill. In F. Giardini & R. Wittek (Eds.), *The Oxford Handbook of Gossip and Reputation* (pp. 173–192). Oxford University Press. https://doi.org/10.1093/oxfordhb/9780190494087.013.10.

McAndrew, F. T., Bell, E. K., & Garcia, C. M. (2007). Who do we tell and whom do we tell on? Gossip as a strategy for status enhancement. *Journal of Applied Social Psychology, 37*(7), 1562–1577. https://doi.org/10.1111/j.1559-1816.2007.00227.x.

Merry, S. E. (1984). Rethinking gossip and scandal. In D. Black (Ed.), *Toward a General Theory of Social Control* (pp. 271–302). Academic Press. https://doi.org/10.1016/B978-0-12-102801-5.50016-9.

Meyers, E. A. (2010). *Gossip Talk and Online Community: Celebrity Gossip Blogs and Their Audiences*. Open Access Dissertations. 292. https://scholarworks.umass.edu/open_access_dissertations/292.

Michel, A. (2011). Transcending socialization: A nine-year ethnography of the body's role in organizational control and knowledge workers' transformation. *Administrative Science Quarterly, 56*(3), 325–368. https://doi.org/10.1177/0001839212437519.

Michelson, G., & Mouly, V. S. (2004). Do loose lips sink ships? The meaning, antecedents and consequences of rumor and gossip in organisations. *Corporate Communications: An International Journal*, *9*(3), 189–201. https://doi.org/10.1108/13563280410551114.

Mielke, A., Preis, A., Samuni, L., et al. (2018). Flexible decision-making in grooming partner choice in sooty mangabeys and chimpanzees. *Royal Society Open Science*, *5*(7), 172143. https://doi.org/10.1098/rsos.172143.

Milgrom, P. R., North, D. C., & Weingast, B. R. (1990). The role of institutions in the revival of trade: The law merchant, private judges, and the champagne fairs. *Economics & Politics*, *2*(1), 1–23. https://doi.org/10.1111/j.1468-0343.1990.tb00020.x.

Milinski, M. (2019). Gossip and reputation in social dilemmas. In F. Giardini & R. Wittek (Eds.), *The Oxford Handbook of Gossip and Reputation* (pp. 193–213). Oxford University Press. https://doi.org/10.1093/oxfordhb/9780190494087.013.11.

Mitra, T., & Gilbert, E. (2012). Have you heard? How gossip flows through workplace email. *Proceedings of the International AAAI Conference on Web and Social Media*, *6*(1), 242–249. https://doi.org/10.1609/icwsm.v6i1.14260.

Moe, W. W., & Schweidel, D. A. (2012). Online product opinions: Incidence, evaluation, and evolution. *Marketing Science*, *31*(3), 372–386. https://doi.org/10.1287/mksc.1110.0662.

Morris, M. W., & Peng, K. (1994). Culture and cause: American and Chinese attributions for social and physical events. *Journal of Personality and Social Psychology*, *67*(6), 949–971. https://doi.org/10.1037/0022-3514.67.6.949.

Mrazek, A. J., Chiao, J. Y., Blizinsky, K. D., Lun, J., & Gelfand, M. J. (2013). The role of culture–gene coevolution in morality judgment: Examining the interplay between tightness–looseness and allelic variation of the serotonin transporter gene. *Culture and Brain*, *1*(2–4), 100–117. https://doi.org/10.1007/s40167-013-0009-x.

Murphy, R. O., Ackermann, K. A., & Handgraaf, M. (2011). Measuring social value orientation. *Judgment and Decision Making*, *6*(8), 771–781. https://doi.org/10.1017/S1930297500004204.

Na, J., Kosinski, M., & Stillwell, D. J. (2015). When a new tool is introduced in different cultural contexts: Individualism–collectivism and social network on Facebook. *Journal of Cross-Cultural Psychology*, *46*(3), 355–370. https://doi.org/10.1177/0022022114563932.

Németh, A., & Takács, K. (2010). The paradox of cooperation benefits. *Journal of Theoretical Biology*, *264*(2), 301–311. https://doi.org/10.1016/j.jtbi.2010.02.005.

Nesse, R. M. (2013). Tinbergen's four questions, organized: A response to Bateson and Laland. *Trends in Ecology & Evolution*, *28*(12), 681–682. https://doi.org/10.1016/j.tree.2013.10.008.

Nesse, R. M. (2019). *Good Reasons for Bad Feelings: Insights from the Frontier of Evolutionary Psychiatry*. Penguin.

Nieper, A. S., Beersma, B., Dijkstra, M. T., & van Kleef, G. A. (2022). When and why does gossip increase prosocial behavior? *Current Opinion in Psychology*, *44*, 315–320. https://doi.org/10.1016/j.copsyc.2021.10.009.

Noë, R., & Hammerstein, P. (1995). Biological markets. *Trends in Ecology & Evolution*, *10*(8), 336–339. https://doi.org/10.1016/S0169-5347(00)89123-5.

Nowak, M. A., & Sigmund, K. (1998). Evolution of indirect reciprocity by image scoring. *Nature*, *393*(6685), 573–577. https://doi.org/10.1038/31225.

Nowak, M. A., & Sigmund, K. (2005). Evolution of indirect reciprocity. *Nature*, *437*(7063), 1291–1298. https://doi.org/10.1038/nature04131.

Nowak, M., & Highfield, R. (2011). *Supercooperators: Altruism, Evolution, and Why We Need Each Other to Succeed*. Simon and Schuster.

Paine, R. (1968). Gossip and transaction. *Man*, *3*(2), 305–308. www.jstor.org/stable/2798510.

Panchanathan, K., & Boyd, R. (2004). Indirect reciprocity can stabilize cooperation without the second-order free rider problem. *Nature*, *432*(7016), 499–502. https://doi.org/10.1038/nature02978.

Piazza, J., & Bering, J. M. (2008). Concerns about reputation via gossip promote generous allocations in an economic game. *Evolution and Human Behavior*, *29* (3), 172–178. https://doi.org/10.1016/j.evolhumbehav.2007.12.002.

Piazza, J., Bering, J. M., & Ingram, G. (2011). “Princess Alice is watching you”: Children’s belief in an invisible person inhibits cheating. *Journal of Experimental Child Psychology*, *109*(3), 311–320. https://doi.org/10.1016/j.jecp.2011.02.003.

Premack, D., & Woodruff, G. (1978). Does the chimpanzee have a theory of mind? *Behavioral and Brain Sciences*, *1*(4), 515–526. https://doi:10.1017/S0140525X00076512.

Przepiorka, W., Norbutas, L., & Corten, R. (2017). Order without law: Reputation promotes cooperation in a cryptomarket for illegal drugs. *European Sociological Review*, *33*(6), 752–764. https://doi.org/10.1093/esr/jcx072.

Puranam, P. (2018). *The Microstructure of Organizations*. Oxford University Press.

Raub, W., & Weesie, J. (1990). Reputation and efficiency in social interactions: An example of network effects. *American Journal of Sociology*, *96*(3), 626–654. https://doi.org/10.1086/229574.

Rehm, M., Rohlfing, K., & Goecke, K. U. (2003). Situatedness: The Interplay between context(s) and situation. *Journal of Cognition and Culture*, *3*(2), 132–156. https://doi.org/10.1163/156853703322148516.

Roberts, G. (1998). Competitive altruism: From reciprocity to the handicap principle. *Proceedings of the Royal Society of London. Series B: Biological Sciences*, *265*(1394), 427–431. https://doi.org/10.1098/rspb.1998.0312.

Roberts, G., Raihani, N., Bshary, R., et al. (2021). The benefits of being seen to help others: Indirect reciprocity and reputation-based partner choice.

Philosophical Transactions of the Royal Society B, *376*(1838), 20200290. https://doi.org/10.1098/rstb.2020.0290.

Santos, F. P., Pacheco, J. M., & Santos, F. C. (2021). The complexity of human cooperation under indirect reciprocity. *Philosophical Transactions of the Royal Society B*, *376*(1838), 20200291. https://doi.org/10.1098/rstb.2020.0291.

Scott, J. C. (2008a). *Domination and the Arts of Resistance*. Yale University Press.

Scott, J. C. (2008b). *Weapons of the Weak*. Yale University Press.

Scott-Phillips, T. C., Dickins, T. E., & West, S. A. (2011). Evolutionary theory and the ultimate–proximate distinction in the human behavioral sciences. *Perspectives on Psychological Science*, *6*(1), 38–47. https://doi.org/10.1177/1745691610393528.

Shaw, A., Montinari, N., Piovesan, M., et al. (2014). Children develop a veil of fairness. *Journal of Experimental Psychology: General*, *143*(1), 363–375. https://doi.org/10.1037/a0031247.

Shenk, D. (1997). *Data Smog*. Harper Collins.

Snijders, C., & Matzat, U. (2019). Online reputation systems. In F. Giardini & R. Wittek (Eds.), *The Oxford Handbook of Gossip and Reputation* (pp. 479–496). Oxford University Press. https://doi.org/10.1093/oxfordhb/9780190494087.013.25.

Soeters, J., & van Iterson, A. (2002). Blame and praise gossip in organizations: Established, outsiders and the civilising process. *Advances in Organization Studies*, *10*, 25–40.

Sommerfeld, R. D., Krambeck, H. J., & Milinski, M. (2008). Multiple gossip statements and their effect on reputation and trustworthiness. *Proceedings of the Royal Society of London B*, *275*, 2529–2536. https://doi.org/10.1098/rspb.2008.0762.

Sommerfeld, R. D., Krambeck, H. J., Semmann, D., & Milinski, M. (2007). Gossip as an alternative for direct observation in games of indirect reciprocity. *Proceedings of the National Academy of Sciences*, *104*(44), 17435–17440. https://doi.org/10.1073/pnas.0704598104.

Steg, L., Lindenberg, S., & Keizer, K. (2016). Intrinsic motivation, norms and environmental behavior: The dynamics of overarching goals. *International Review of Environmental and Resource Economics*, *9*(1–2), 179–207. https://doi.org/10.1561/101.00000077.

Stiff, C. (2019). The Dark Triad and Facebook surveillance: How Machiavellianism, psychopathy, but not narcissism predict using Facebook to spy on others. *Computers in Human Behavior*, *94*, 62–69. https://doi.org/10.1016/j.chb.2018.12.044.

Stirling, R. B. (1956). Some psychological mechanisms operative in gossip. *Social Forces*, *34*(3), 262–267. https://doi.org/10.2307/2574050.

Suls, J. M. (1977). Gossip as social comparison. *Journal of Communication*, *27* (1), 164–168. https://doi.org/10.1111/j.1460-2466.1977.tb01812.x.

Summers, C. H., Korzan, W. J., Lukkes, J. L., et al. (2005). Does Serotonin influence aggression? Comparing regional activity before and during social interaction. *Physiological and Biochemical Zoology*, *78*(5), 679–694. https://doi.org/10.1086/432139.

Tadelis, S. (2016). Reputation and feedback systems in online platform markets. *Annual Review of Economics*, *8*, 321–340. https://doi.org/10.1146/annurev-economics-080315-015325.

Takács, K., Gross, J., Testori, M., et al. (2021). Networks of reliable reputations and cooperation: A review. *Philosophical Transactions of the Royal Society B*, *376*(1838), 20200297. https://doi.org/10.1098/rstb.2020.0297.

Tan, N., Yam, K. C., Zhang, P., & Brown, D. J. (2021). Are you gossiping about me? The costs and benefits of high workplace gossip prevalence. *Journal of Business and Psychology*, *36*(3), 417–434. https://doi.org/10.1007/s10869-020-09683-7.

Tennie, C., Frith, U., & Frith, C. D. (2010). Reputation management in the age of the world-wide web. *Trends in Cognitive Sciences*, *14*(11), 482–488. https://doi.org/10.1016/j.tics.2010.07.003.

Testori, M., Hemelrijk, C. K., & Beersma, B. (2022). Gossip promotes cooperation only when it is pro-socially motivated. *Scientific Reports*, *12*(1), 1–12. https://doi.org/10.1038/s41598-022-08670-7.

Tinbergen, N. (1963). On aims and methods of ethology. *Zeitschrift für Tierpsychologie*, *20*(4), 410–433. https://doi.org/10.1111/j.1439-0310.1963.tb01161.x.

Tomasello, M., & Vaish, A. (2013). Origins of human cooperation and morality. *Annual Review of Psychology*, *64*, 231–255. https://doi.org/10.1146/annurev-psych-113011-143812.

Tomasello, M., Carpenter, M., Call, J., Behne, T., & Moll, H. (2005). Understanding and sharing intentions: The origins of cultural cognition. *Behavioral and Brain Sciences*, *28*(5), 675–691. https://doi.org/10.1017/S0140525X05000129.

Tomasello, M., Melis, A. P., Tennie, C., Wyman, E., & Herrmann, E. (2012). Two key steps in the evolution of human cooperation: The interdependence hypothesis. *Current Anthropology*, *53*(6), 673–692.

Triandis, H. C. (2001). Individualism-collectivism and personality. *Journal of Personality*, *69*(6), 907–924. https://doi.org/10.1111/1467-6494.696169.

Uzzi, B. (1996). The sources and consequences of embeddedness for the economic performance of organizations: The network effect. *American Sociological Review, 61*(4), 674–698. https://doi.org/10.2307/2096399.

Vaidyanathan, B., Khalsa, S., & Ecklund, E. H. (2016). Gossip as social control: Informal sanctions on ethical violations in scientific workplaces. *Social Problems, 63*(4), 554–572. https://doi.org/10.1093/socpro/spw022.

Vaillancourt, T. (2013). Do human females use indirect aggression as an intrasexual competition strategy? *Philosophical Transactions Royal Society B, 368*, 1–7. http://doi.org/10.1098/rstb.2013.0080.

Van Iterson, A., & Clegg, S. R. (2008). The politics of gossip and denial in interorganizational relations. *Human Relations, 61*(8), 1117–1137. https://doi.org/10.1177/0018726708094862.

Van Lange, P. A. (1999). The pursuit of joint outcomes and equality in outcomes: An integrative model of social value orientation. *Journal of Personality and Social Psychology, 77*(2), 337–349. https://doi.org/10.1037/0022-3514.77.2.337.

Villatoro, D., Giardini, F., & Conte, R. (2011). Reputation spreading as sanctioning mechanism for social norm establishment. *Proceedings of the 2nd International Conference on Reputation,* 1–11. https://tinyurl.com/36c4y5f9.

Völker, B., & Flap, H. (2001). Weak ties as a liability: The case of East Germany. *Rationality and Society, 13*(4), 397–428. https://doi.org/10.1177/104346301013004001.

Waddington, K., & Fletcher, C. (2005). Gossip and emotion in nursing and health-care organizations. *Journal of Health Organization and Management, 19*(4/5), 378–394. https://doi.org/10.1108/14777260510615404.

Watkins, S. C., & Danzi, A. D. (1995). Women's gossip and social change: Childbirth and fertility control among Italian and Jewish women in the United States, 1920–1940. *Gender & Society, 9*(4), 469–490. https://doi.org/10.1177/089124395009004005.

Weinberg-Wolf, H., & Chang, S. W. C. (2019). Differences in how macaques monitor others: Does serotonin play a central role? *WIREs Cognitive Science, 10*(4), 1–25. https://doi.org/10.1002/wcs.1494.

Werner, R. M., & Asch, D. A. (2005). The unintended consequences of publicly reporting quality information. *JAMA, 293*(10), 1239–1244. https://doi.org/10.1001/jama.293.10.1239.

Wert, S. R., & Salovey, P. (2004). A social comparison account of gossip. *Review of General Psychology, 8*(2), 122–137. https://doi.org/10.1037/1089-2680.8.2.122.

Wickham, C. (1998). Gossip and resistance among the medieval peasantry. *Past & Present, 160*, 3–24. https://doi.org/10.1093/past/160.1.3.

Wilson, D. S. (1992). Complex interactions in metacommunities, with implications for biodiversity and higher levels of selection. *Ecology, 73*(6), 1984–2000. https://doi.org/10.2307/1941449.

Wilson, D. S. (1998). Adaptive individual differences within single populations. *Philosophical Transactions of the Royal Society B: Biological Sciences, 353* (1366), 199–205. https://doi.org/10.1098/rstb.1998.0202.

Wilson, D. S., & Wilson, E. O. (2008). Evolution "for the Good of the Group." *American Scientist, 96*(5), 380–389. www.jstor.org/stable/27859205.

Wilson, D. S., Near, D. C., & Miller, R. R. (1998). Individual differences in Machiavellianism as a mix of cooperative and exploitative strategies. *Evolution and Human Behavior, 19*(3), 203–212. https://doi.org/10.1016/S1090-5138(98)00011-7.

Wilson, D. S., Near, D., & Miller, R. R. (1996). Machiavellianism: A synthesis of the evolutionary and psychological literatures. *Psychological Bulletin, 119* (2), 285–299. https://doi.org/10.1037/0033-2909.119.2.285.

Wilson, D. S., O'Brien, D. T., & Sesma, A. (2009). Human prosociality from an evolutionary perspective: Variation and correlations at a city-wide scale. *Evolution and Human Behavior, 30*(3), 190–200. https://doi.org/10.1016/j.evolhumbehav.2008.12.002.

Wilson, D. S., Van Vugt, M., & O'Gorman, R. (2008). Multilevel selection theory and major evolutionary transitions: Implications for psychological science. *Current Directions in Psychological Science, 17*(1), 6–9. https://doi.org/10.1111/j.1467-8721.2008.00538.x.

Wilson, D. S., Wilczynski, C., Wells, A., & Weiser, L. (2000). Gossip and other aspects of language as group-level adaptations. In L. Huber & C. M. Heyes (Eds.), *The Evolution of Cognition* (347–366). MIT Press.

Wilson, H. L. (1910). Latin Inscriptions at the Johns Hopkins University. IV. *The American Journal of Philology, 31*(1), 25–42. https://doi.org/10.2307/288847.

Wittek, R. (2013). Norm violations and informal control in organizations: A relational signaling perspective. In B. Nooteboom & F. Six (Eds.), *The Trust Process in Organizations: Empirical Studies of the Determinants and the Process of Trust Development* (pp. 168–195). Edward Elgar. https://doi.org/10.4337/9781843767350.00015.

Wittek, R., & Wielers, R. (1998). Gossip in organizations. *Computational & Mathematical Organization Theory, 4*(2), 189–204. https://doi.org/10.1023/A:1009636325582.

Wittek, R., Snijders, T., & Nee, V. (2013). Introduction: Rational choice social research. In R. Wittek, T. A. B. Snijders, & V. Nee (Eds), *The Handbook of Rational Choice Social Research* (pp. 1–32). Stanford University Press.

Wu, J., Balliet, D., & Van Lange, P. A. (2016). Reputation, gossip, and human cooperation. *Social and Personality Psychology Compass*, *10*(6), 350–364. https://doi.org/10.1111/spc3.12255.

Xiao, Z., & Tsui, A. S. (2007). When brokers may not work: The cultural contingency of social capital in Chinese high-tech firms. *Administrative Science Quarterly*, *52*(1), 1–31. https://doi.org/10.2189/asqu.52.1.1.

Yoeli, E., Hoffman, M., Rand, D. G., & Nowak, M. A. (2013). Powering up with indirect reciprocity in a large-scale field experiment. *Proceedings of the National Academy of Sciences*, *110*, 10424–10429. https://doi.org/10.1073/pnas.130121011.

Acknowledgments

This study is part of the research program *Sustainable Cooperation – Roadmaps to Resilient Societies* (SCOOP). Rafael Wittek gratefully acknowledges funding from the Dutch Organization for Scientific Research (NWO 2017 Gravitation Program, grant number 024.003.025), and from the *Royal Netherlands Institute in Rome* (KNIR; grant number 2022-U-0088). We thank Siegwart Lindenberg for guidance and constructive feedback on an earlier draft of this manuscript, and are grateful to the series editor, David Bjorklund, and two anonymous reviewers for their valuable suggestions. Remaining errors are our own.

Cambridge Elements

Applied Evolutionary Science

David F. Bjorklund
Florida Atlantic University

David F. Bjorklund is a Professor of Psychology at Florida Atlantic University in Boca Raton, Florida. He is the Editor-in-Chief of the *Journal of Experimental Child Psychology*, the Vice President of the Evolution Institute, and has written numerous articles and books on evolutionary developmental psychology, with a particular interest in the role of immaturity in evolution and development.

Editorial Board

About the Series

This series presents original, concise, and authoritative reviews of key topics in applied evolutionary science. Highlighting how an evolutionary approach can be applied to real-world social issues, many Elements in this series will include findings from programs that have produced positive educational, social, economic, or behavioral benefits. Cambridge Elements in Applied Evolutionary Science is published in association with the Evolution Institute.

Cambridge Elements

Applied Evolutionary Science

Elements in the Series

Improving Breastfeeding Rates: Evolutionary Anthropological Insights for Public Health
Emily H. Emmott

The Hidden Talents Framework: Implications for Science, Policy, and Practice
Bruce J. Ellis, Laura S. Abrams, Ann S. Masten, Robert J. Sternberg, Nim Tottenham and Willem E. Frankenhuis

An Introduction to Positive Evolutionary Psychology
Glenn Geher, Megan Fritche, Avrey Goodwine, Julia Lombard, Kaitlyn Longo and Darcy Montana

Superorganism: Toward a New Social Contract for Our Endangered Species
Peter A. Corning

The Evolution of Reputation-Based Cooperation: A Goal Framing Theory of Gossip
Rafael Wittek and Francesca Giardini

A full series listing is available at: www.cambridge.org/EAES

Printed in the United States
by Baker & Taylor Publisher Services